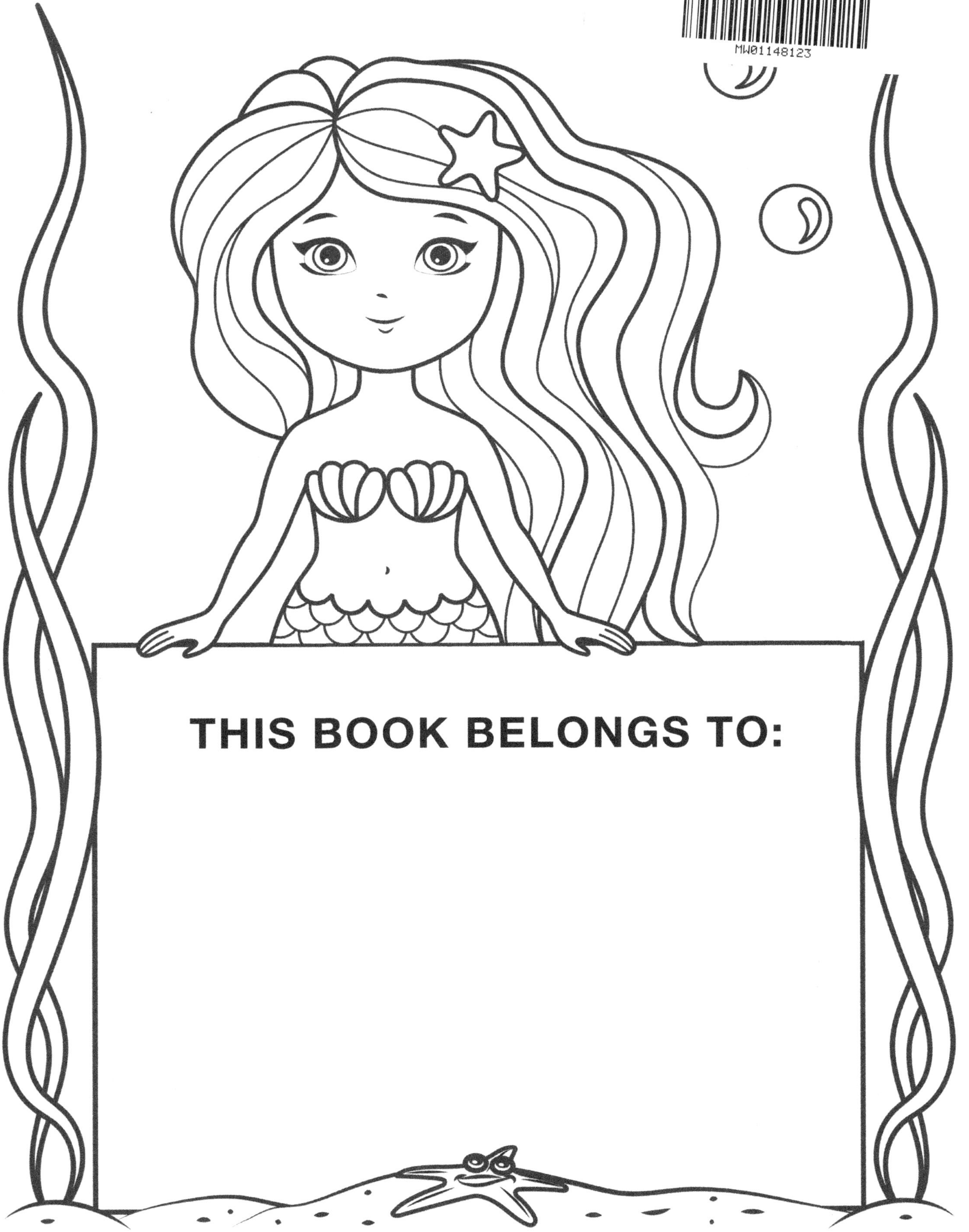
THIS BOOK BELONGS TO:

Illustrated by: C.L. Kozun
Book Design & Editing: Barbara House

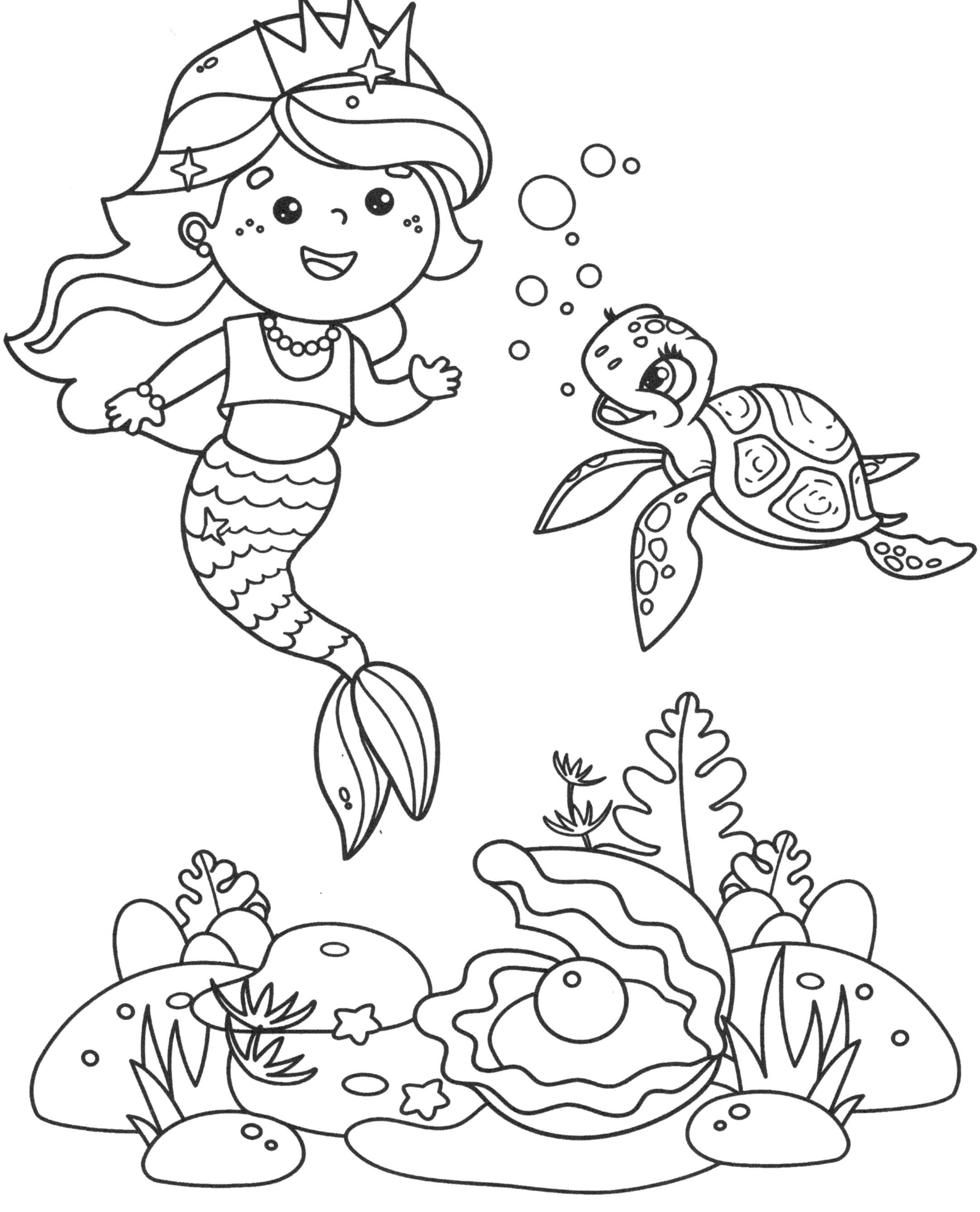

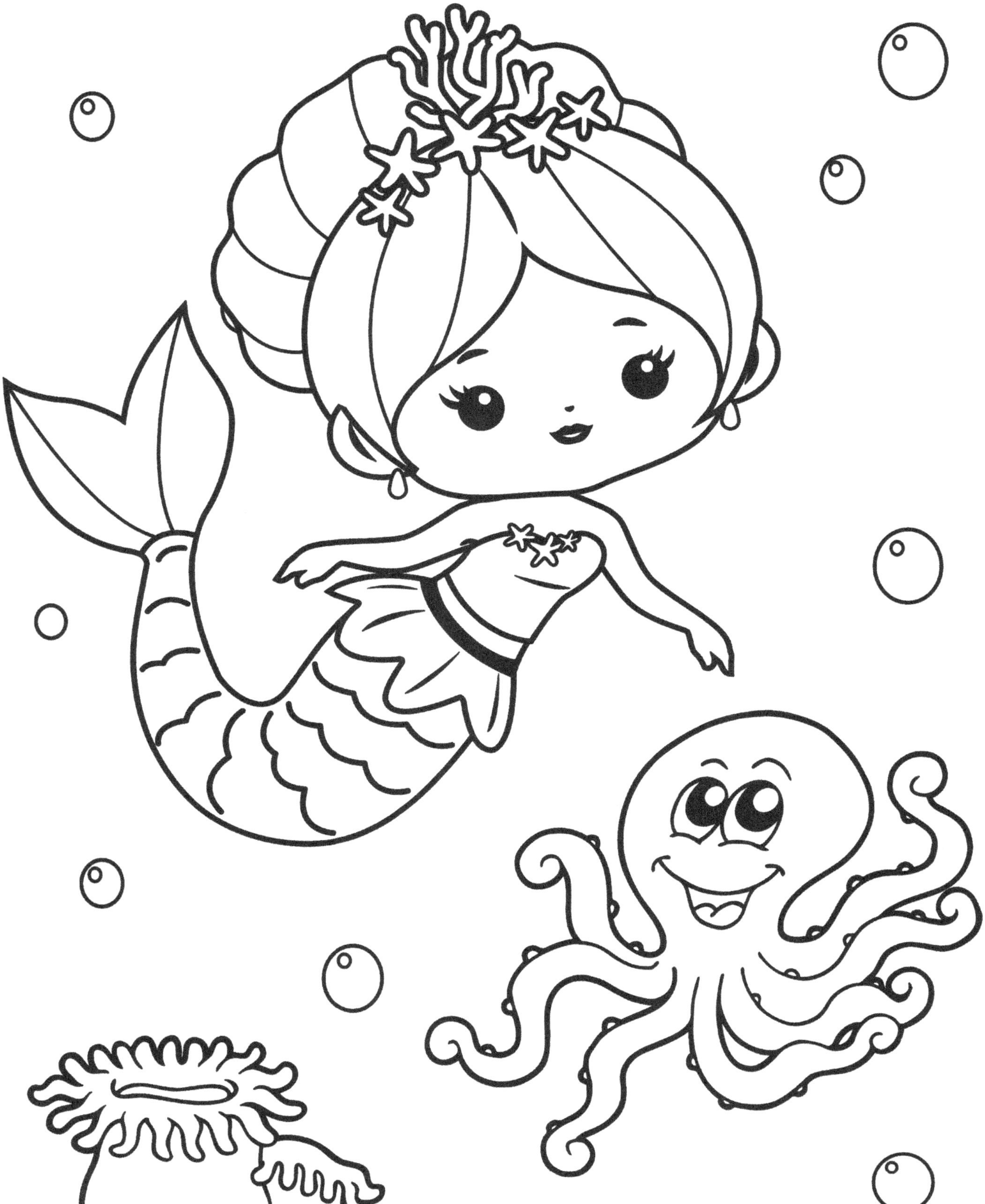

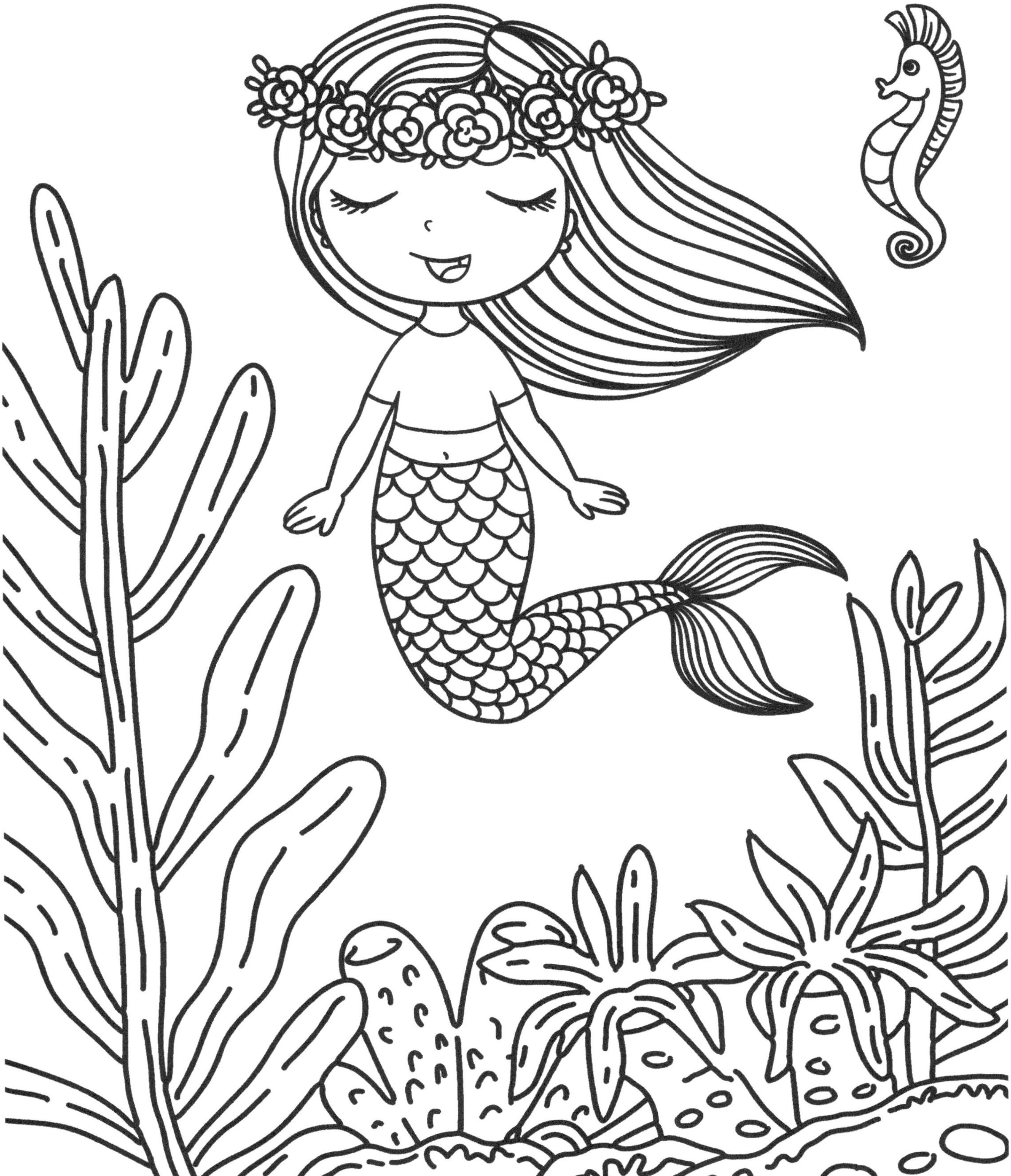

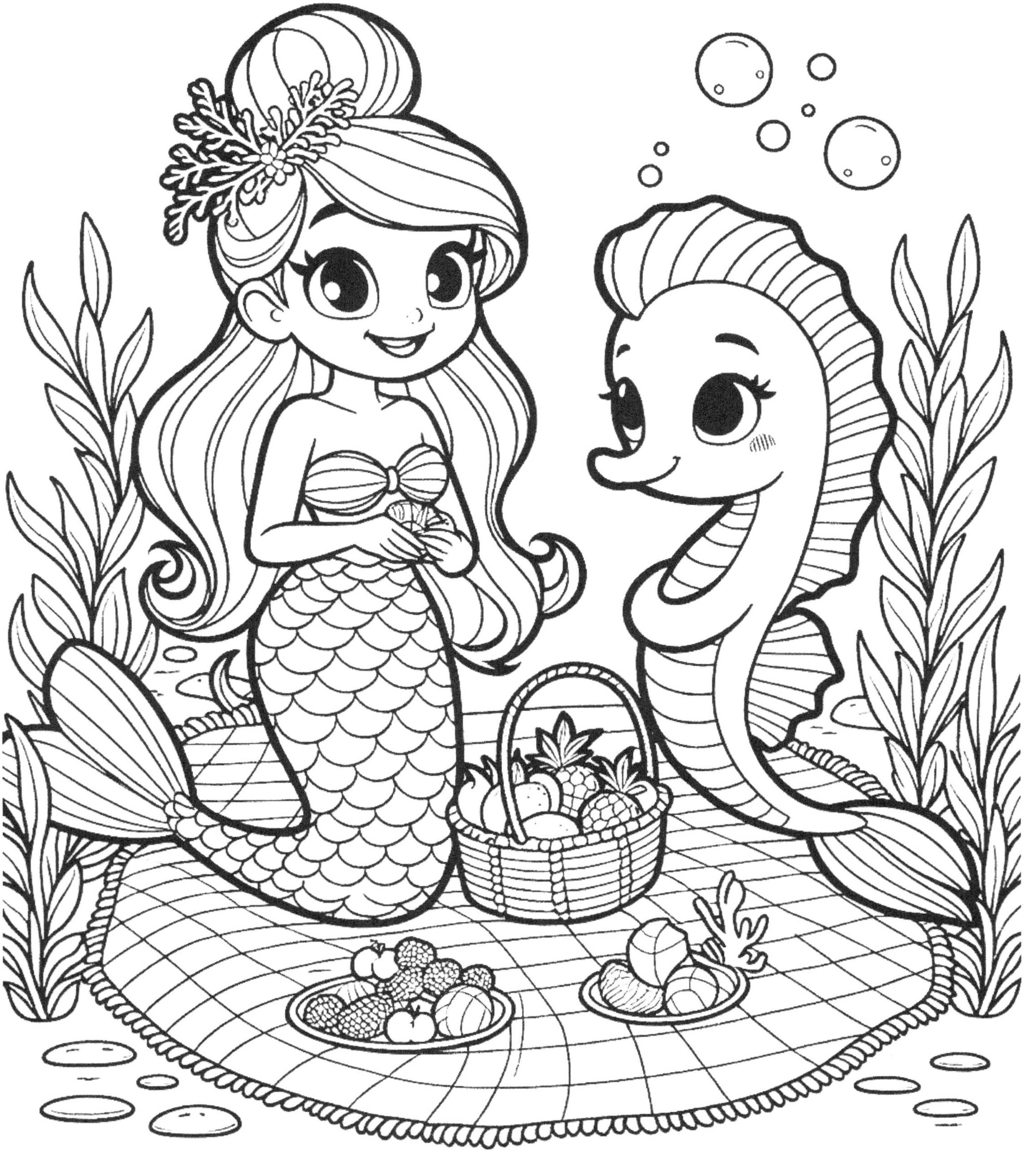

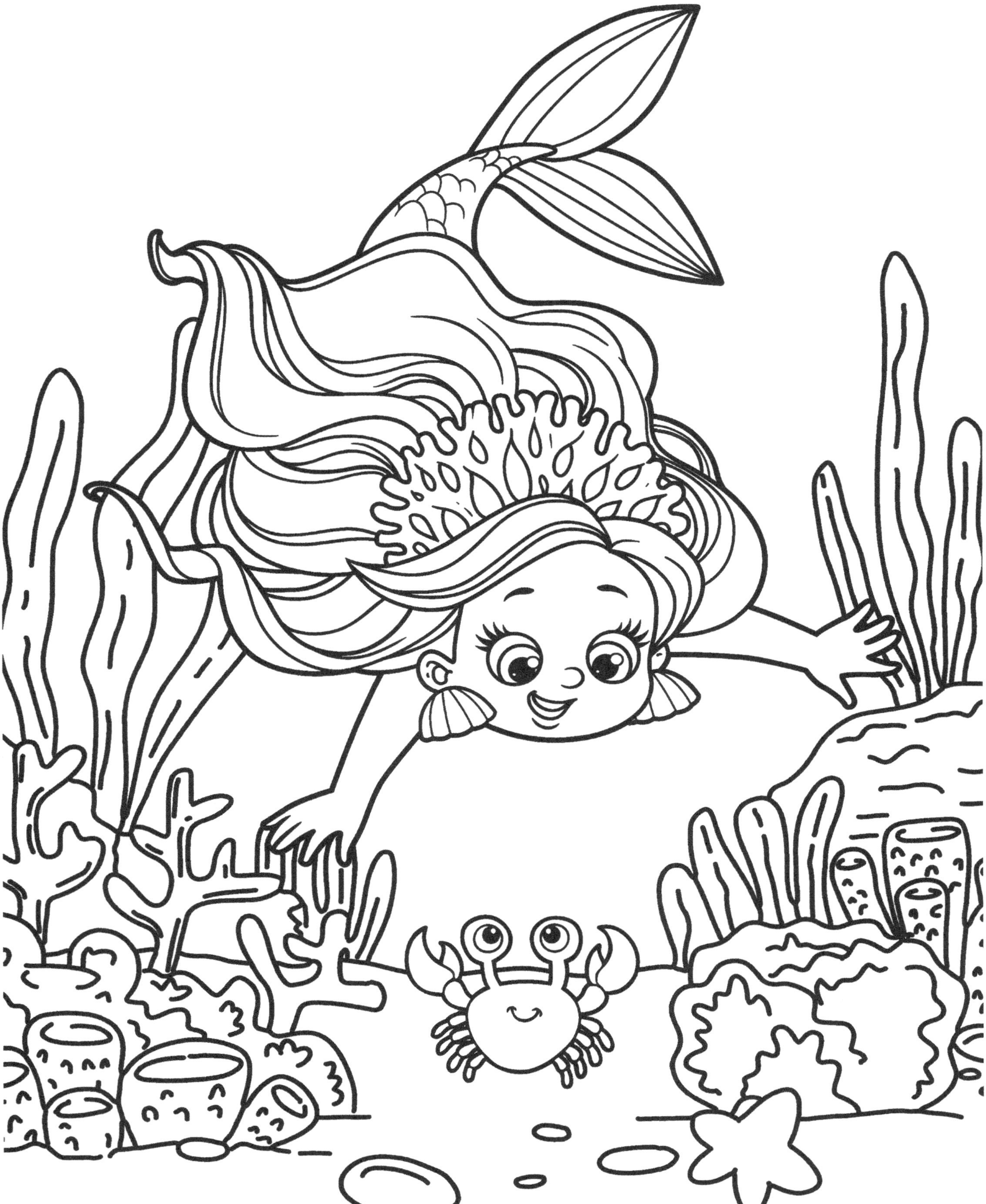

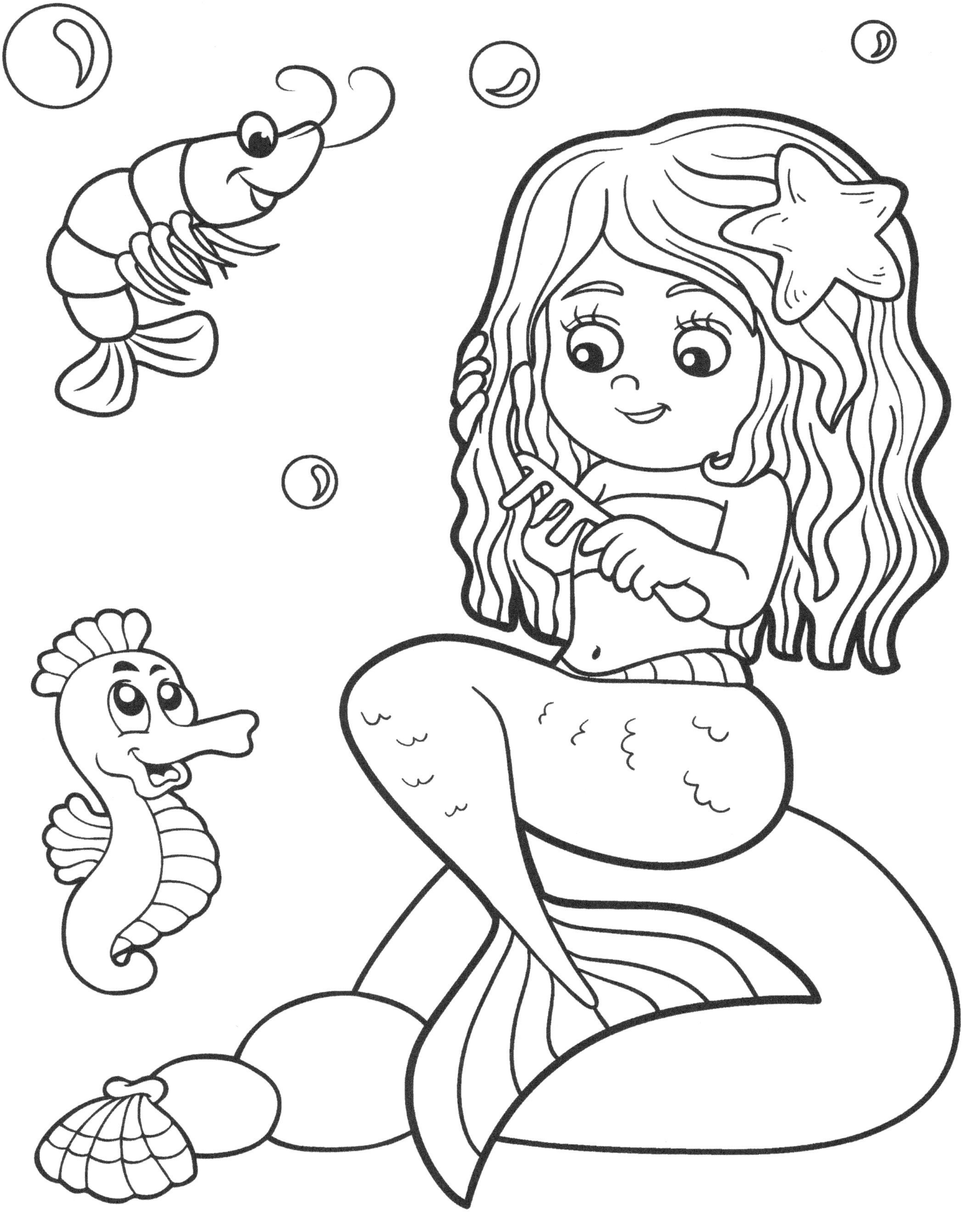

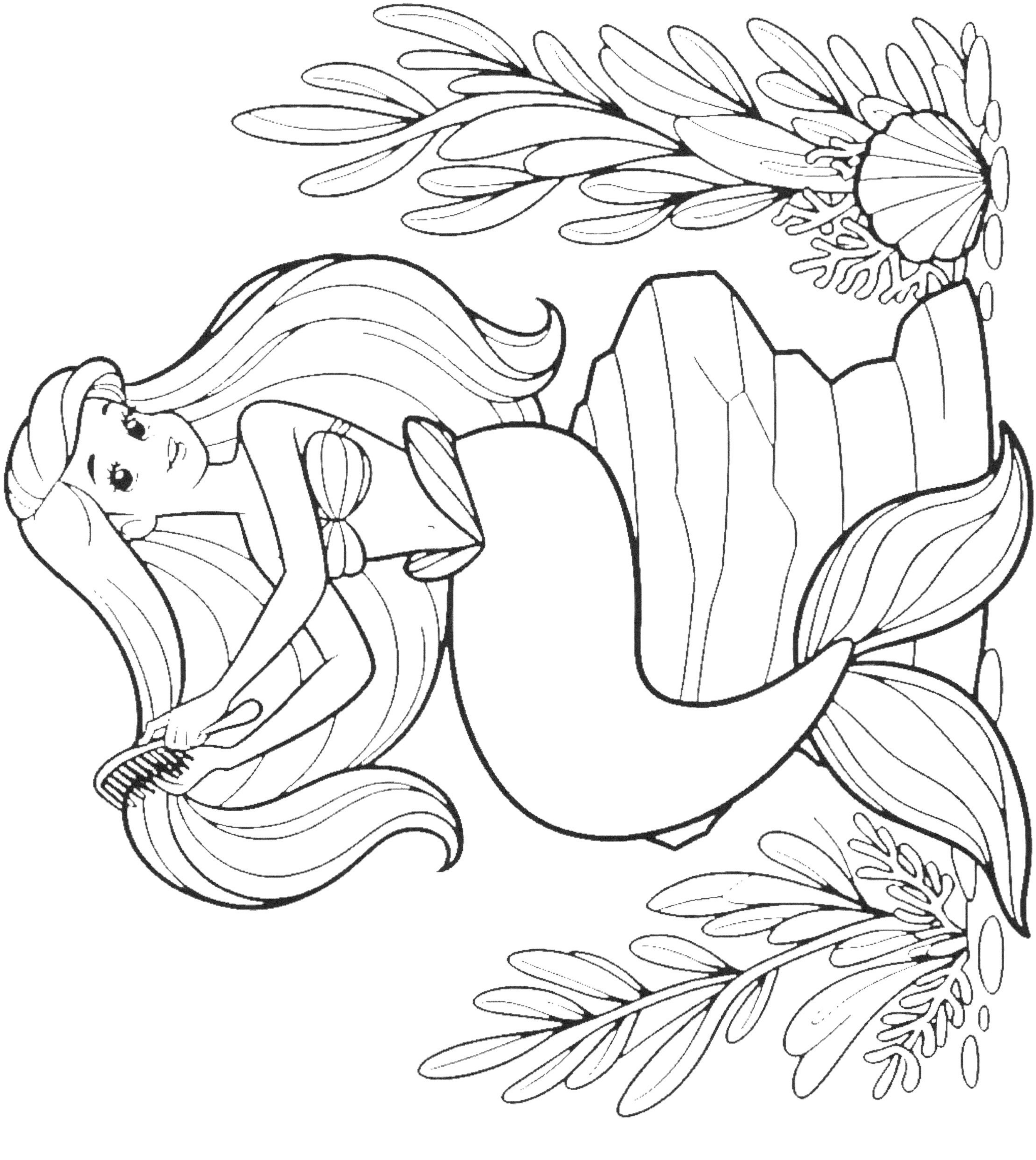

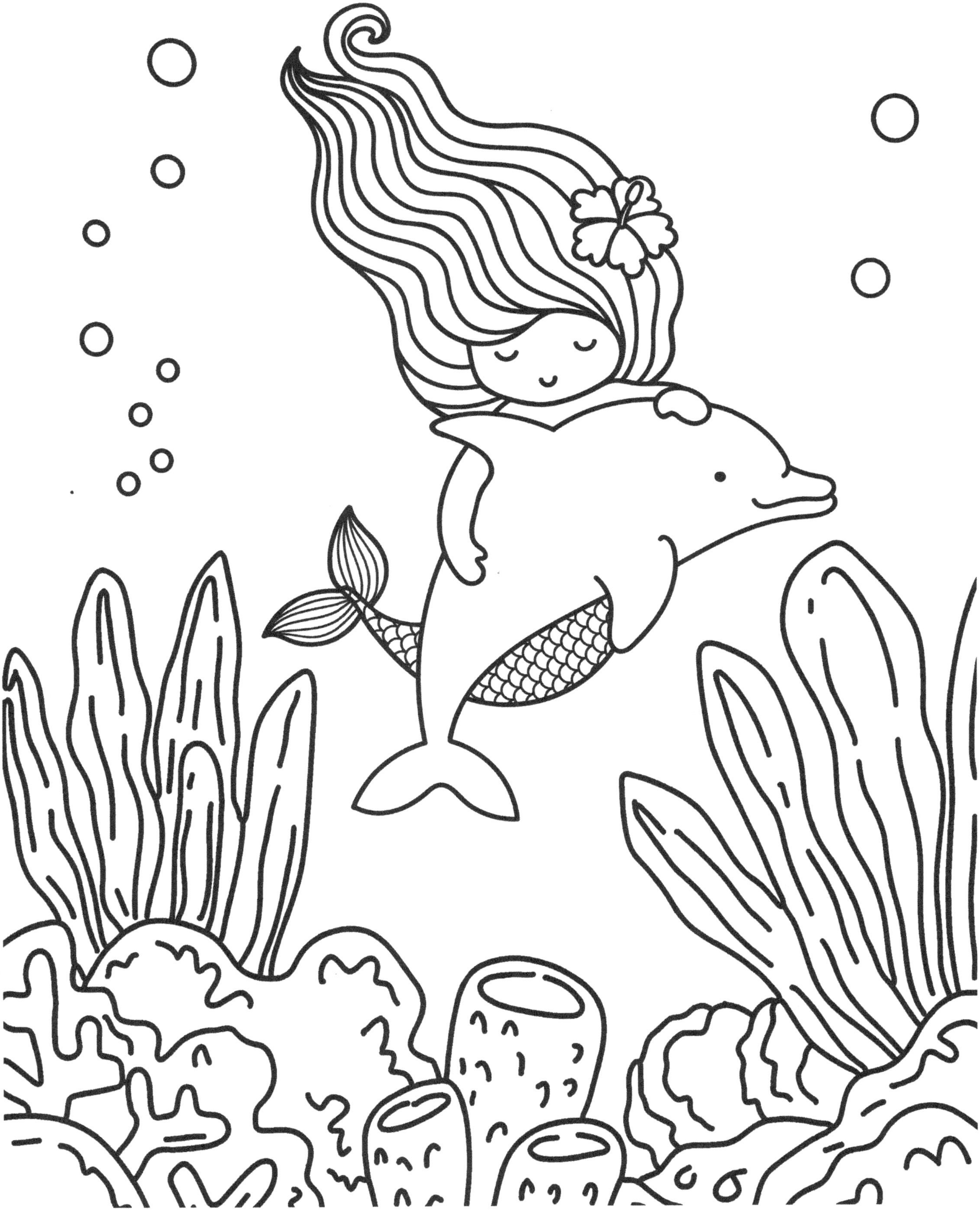

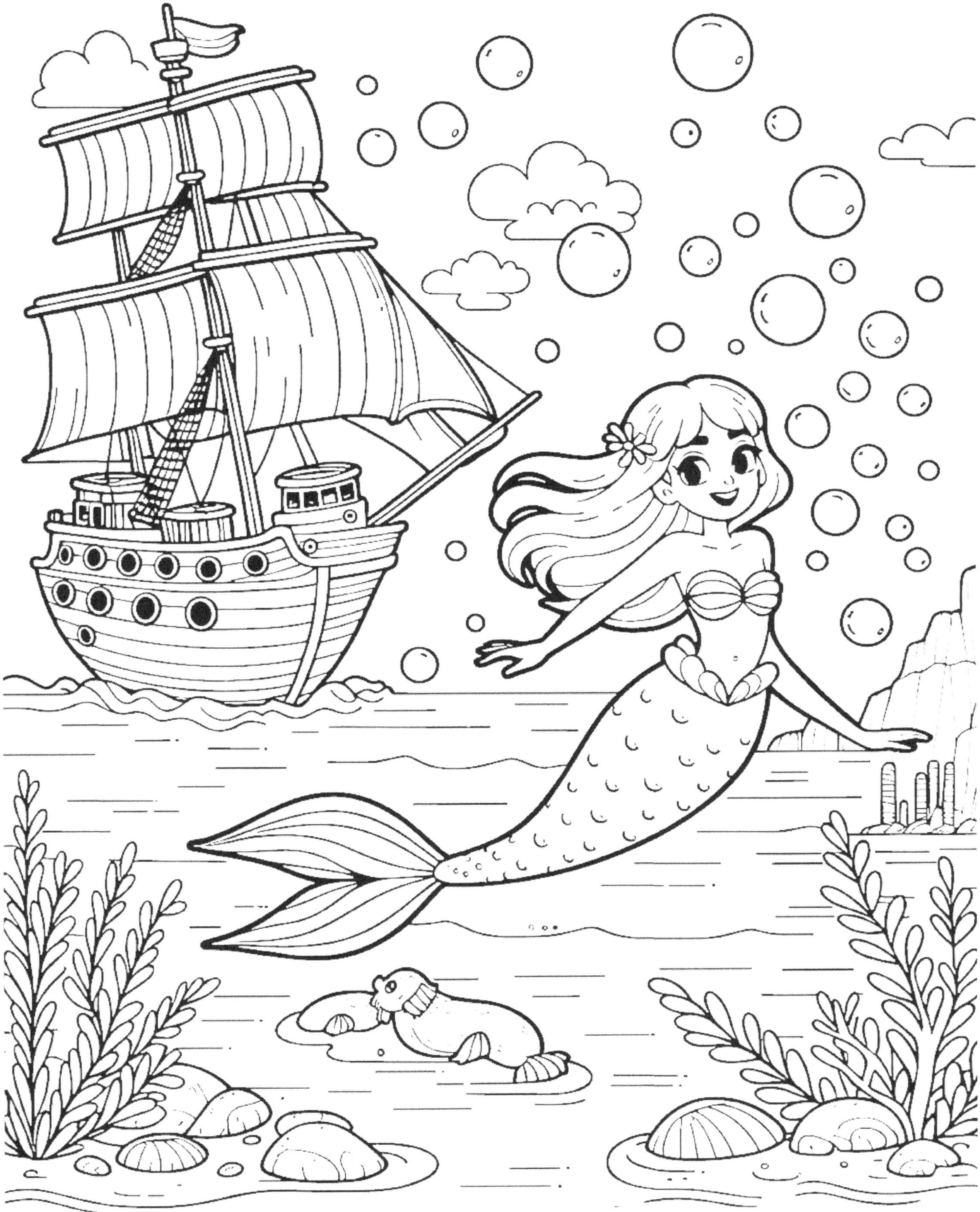

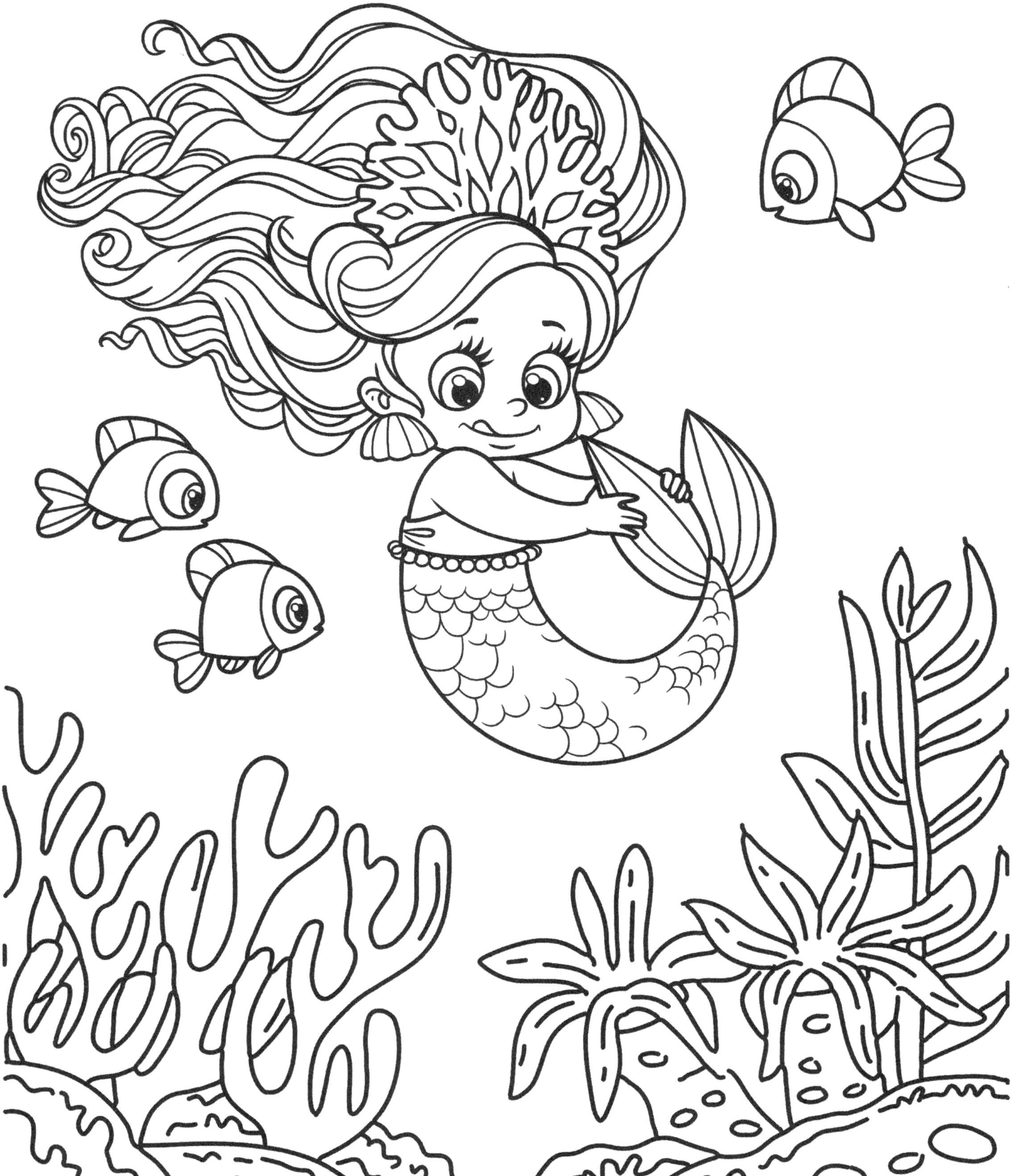

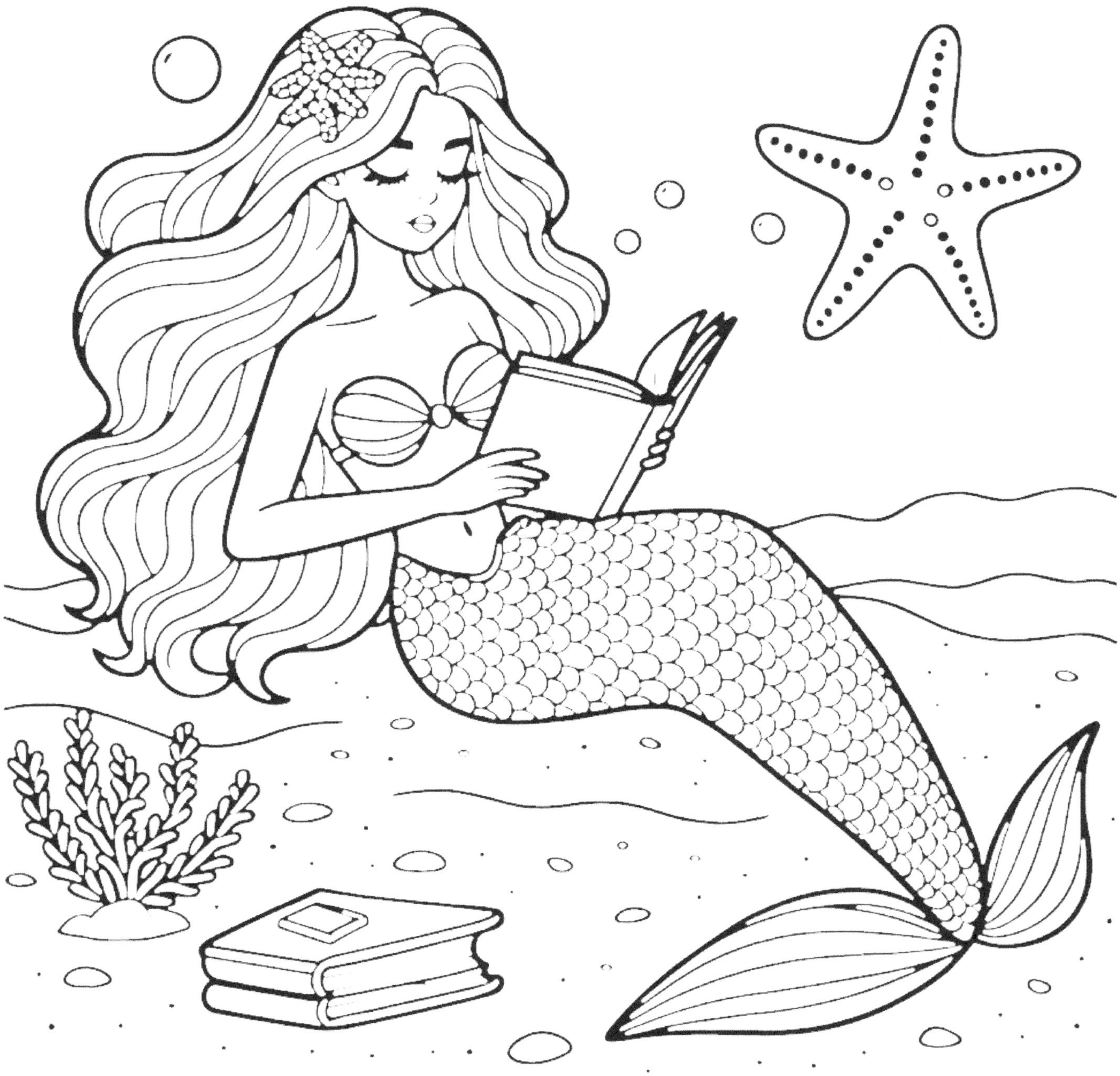

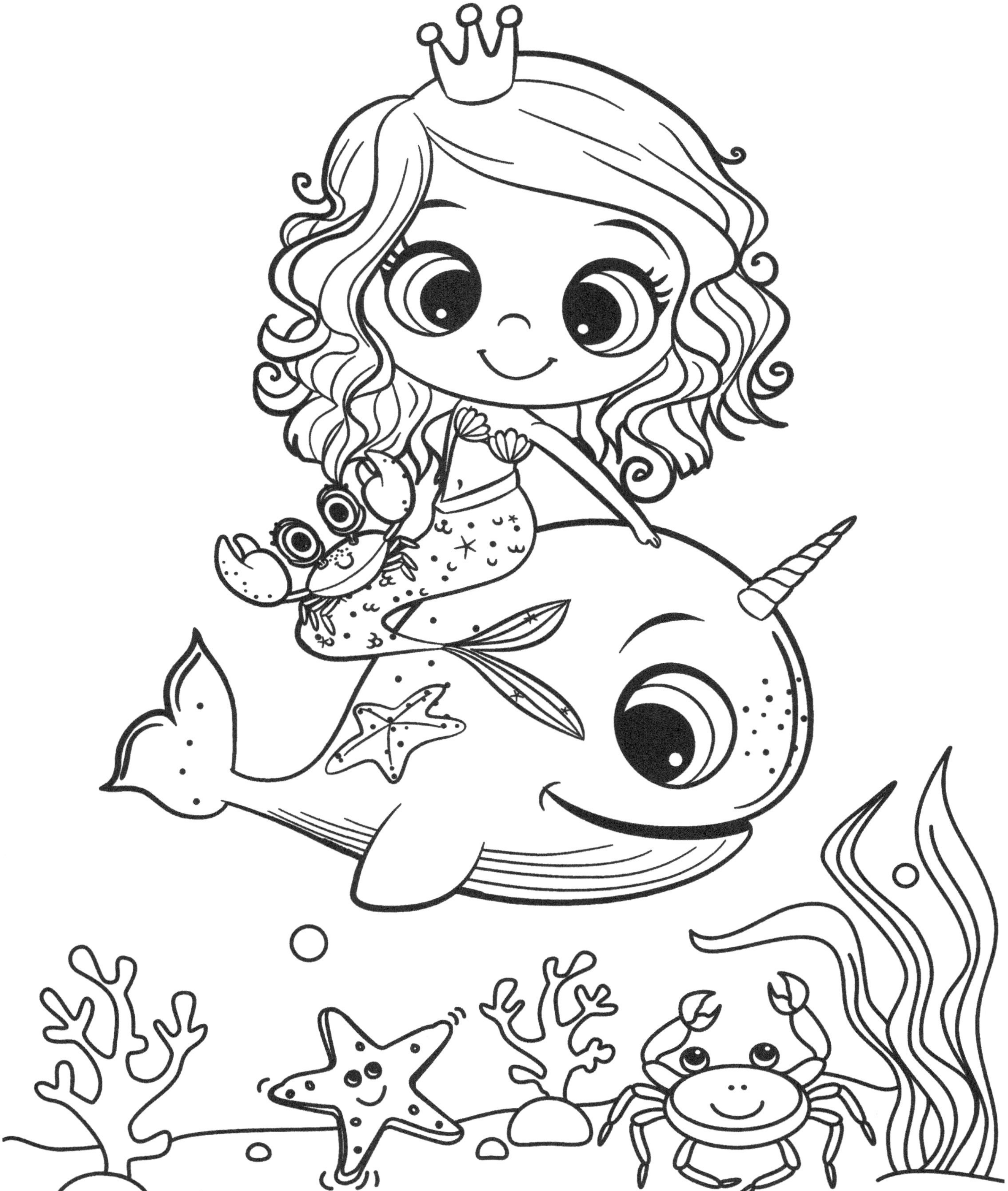

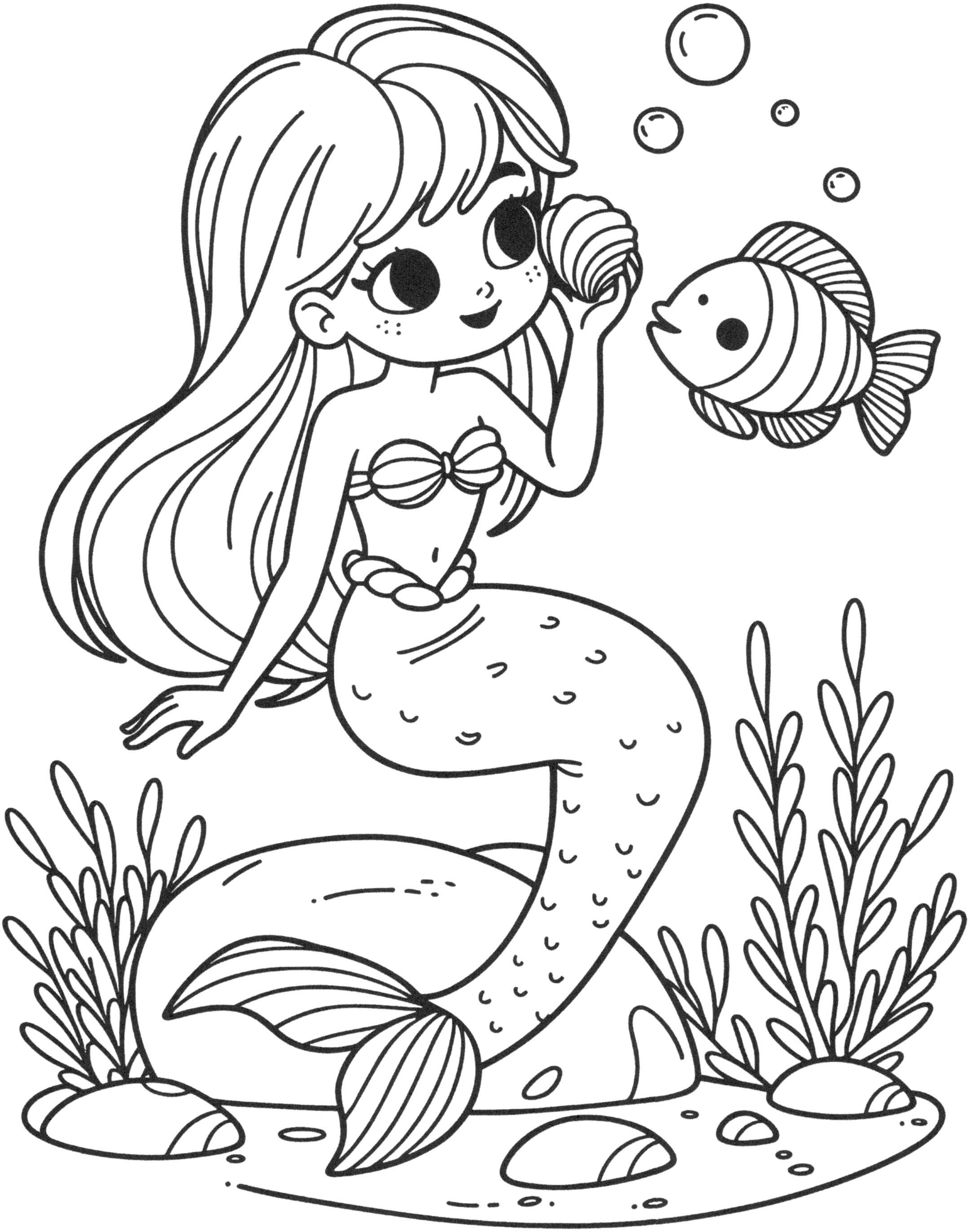

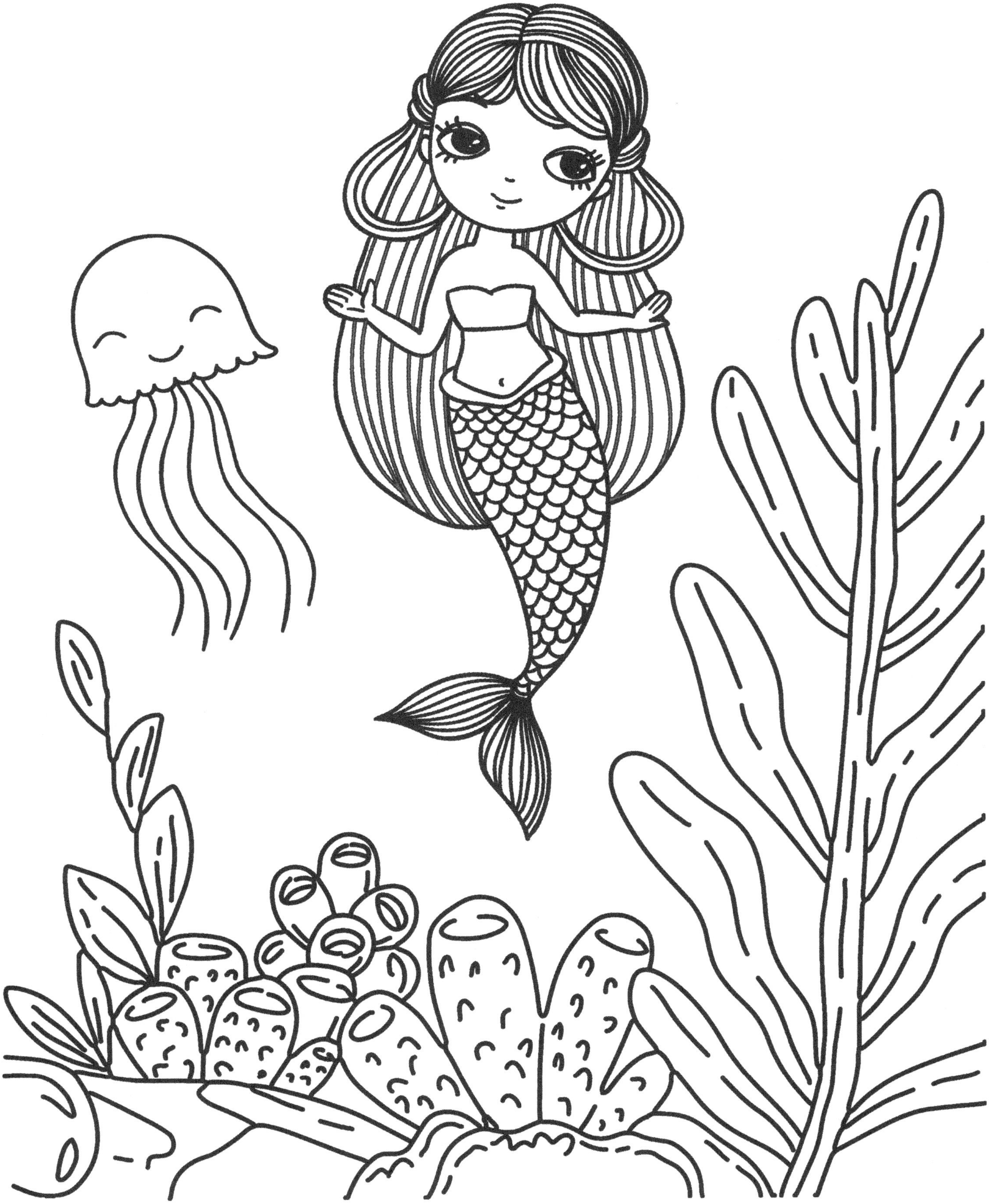

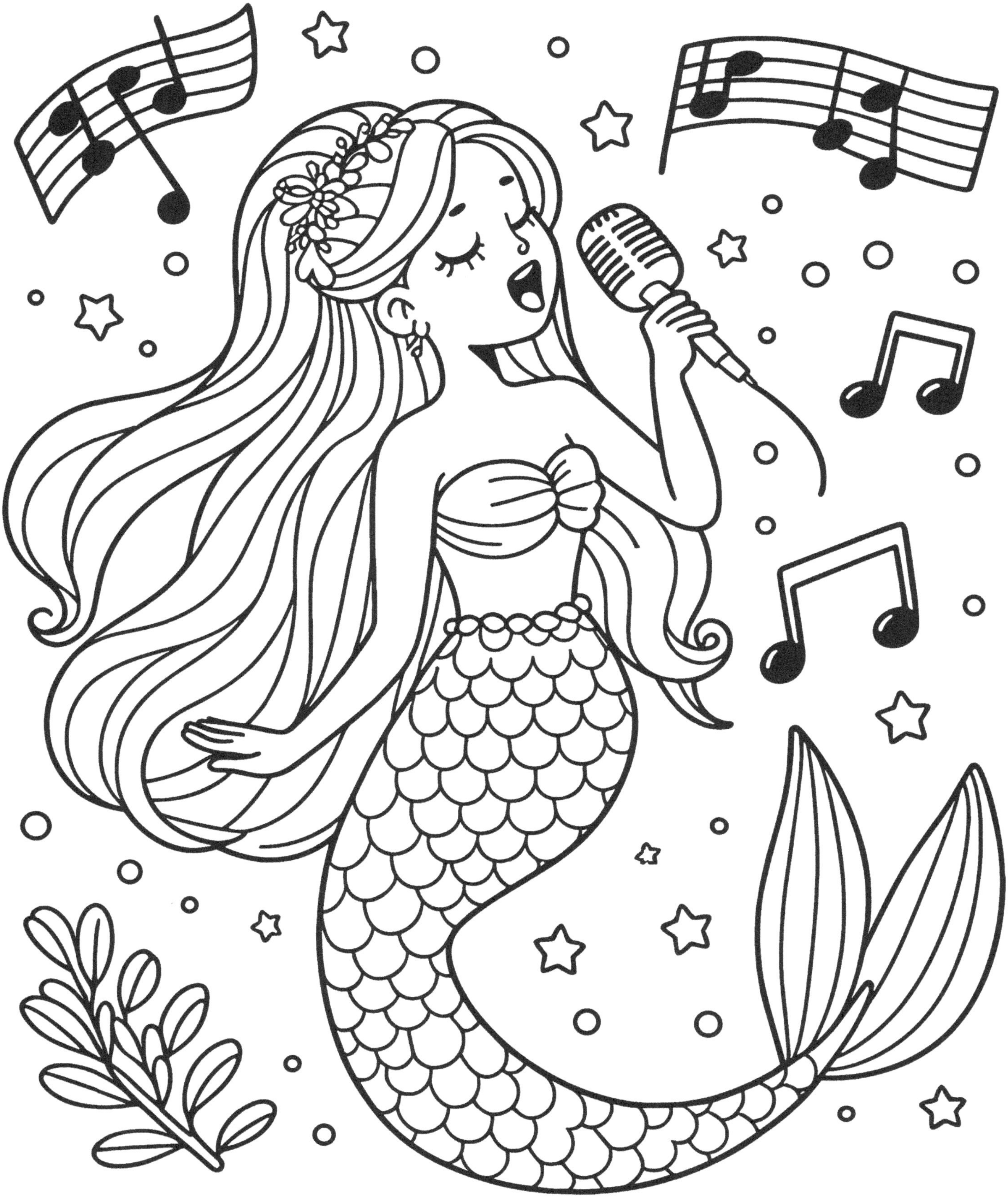

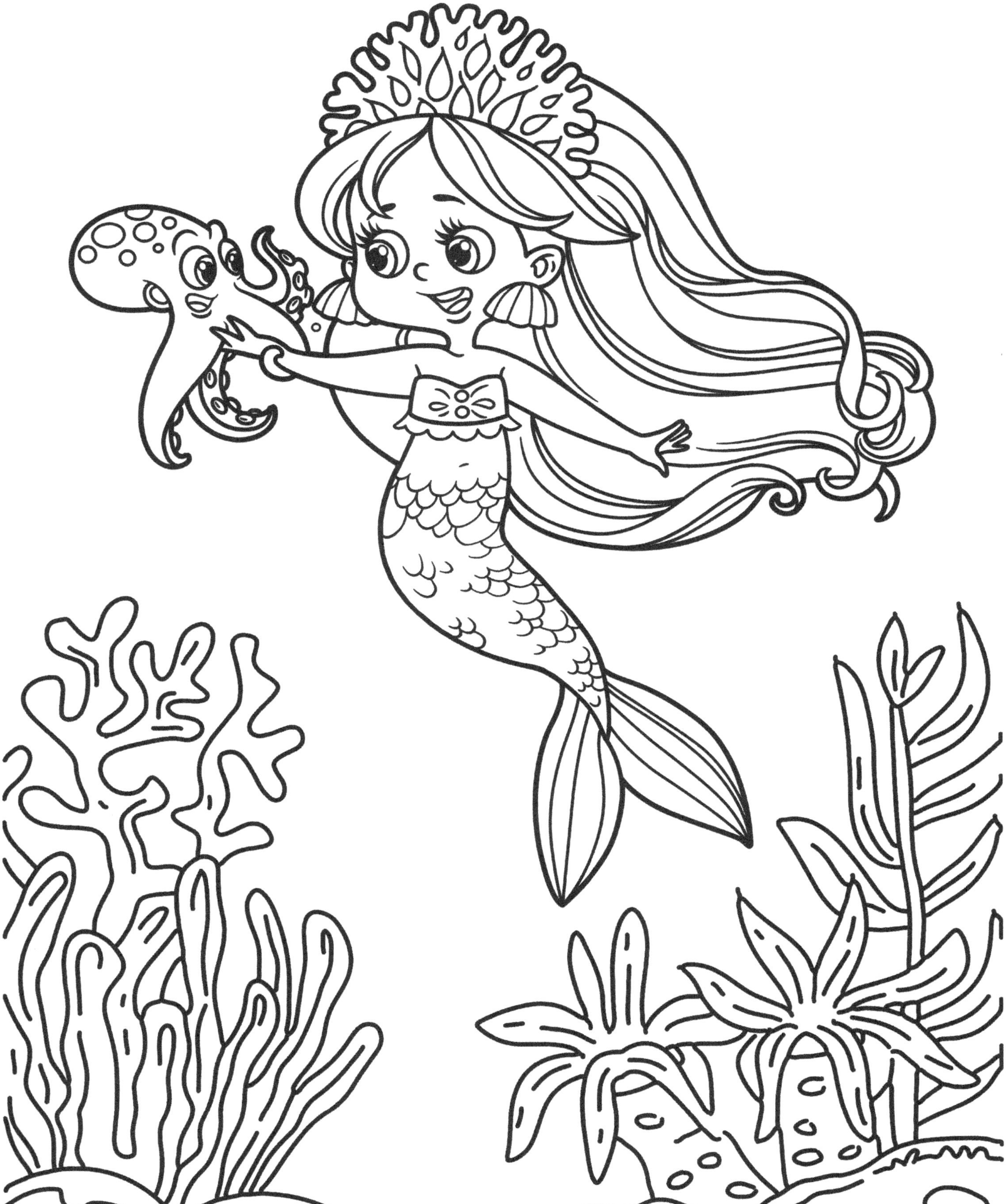

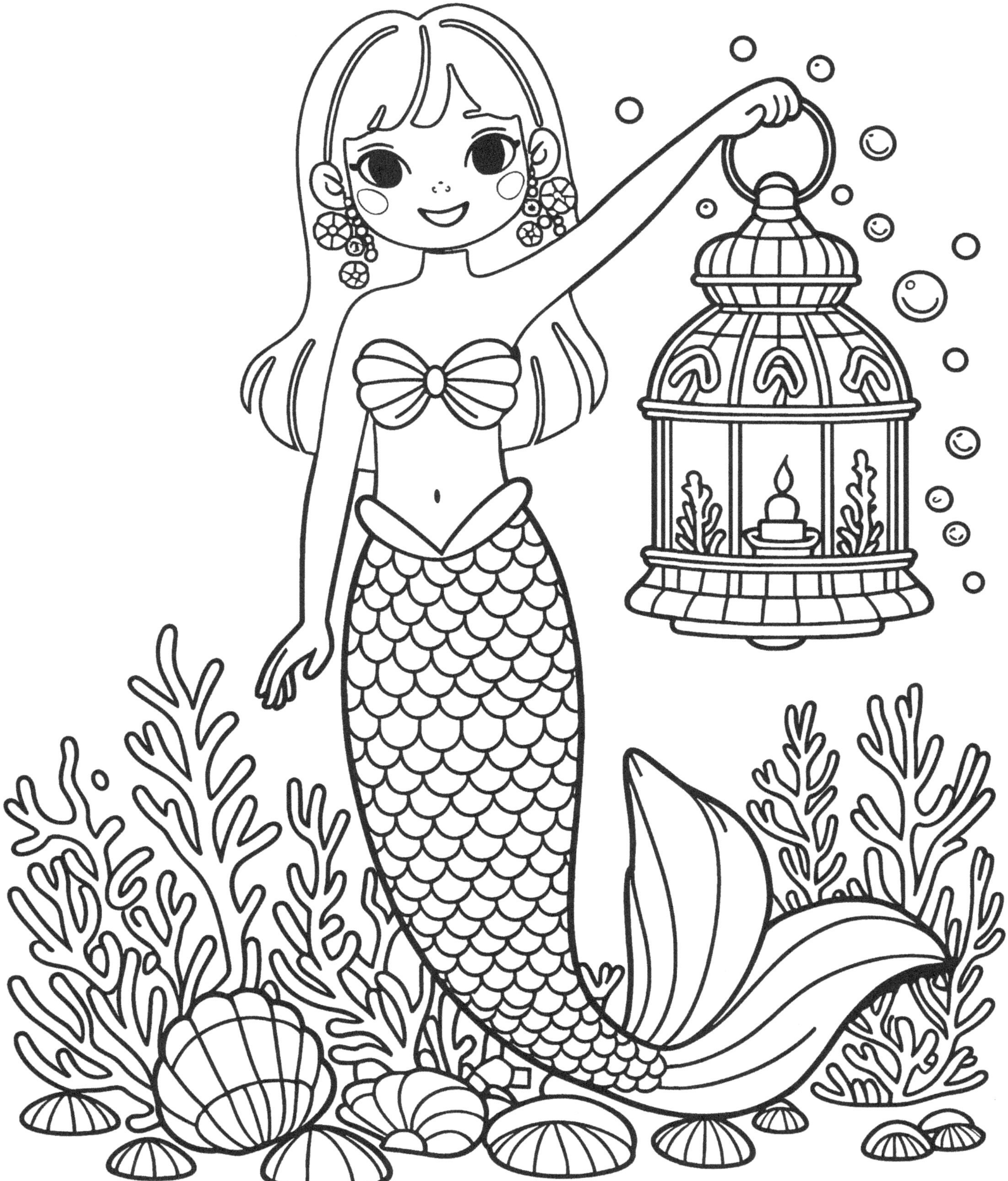

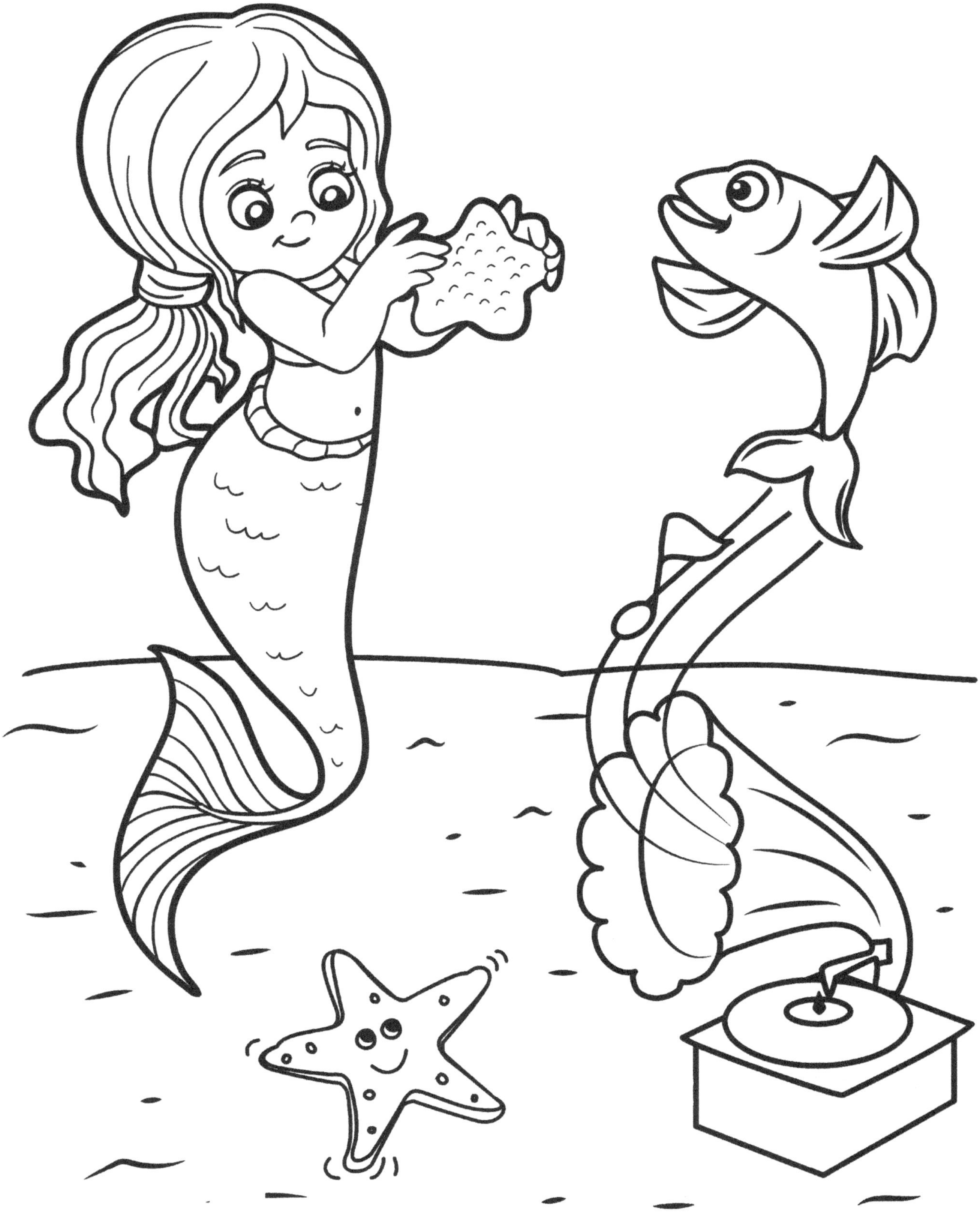

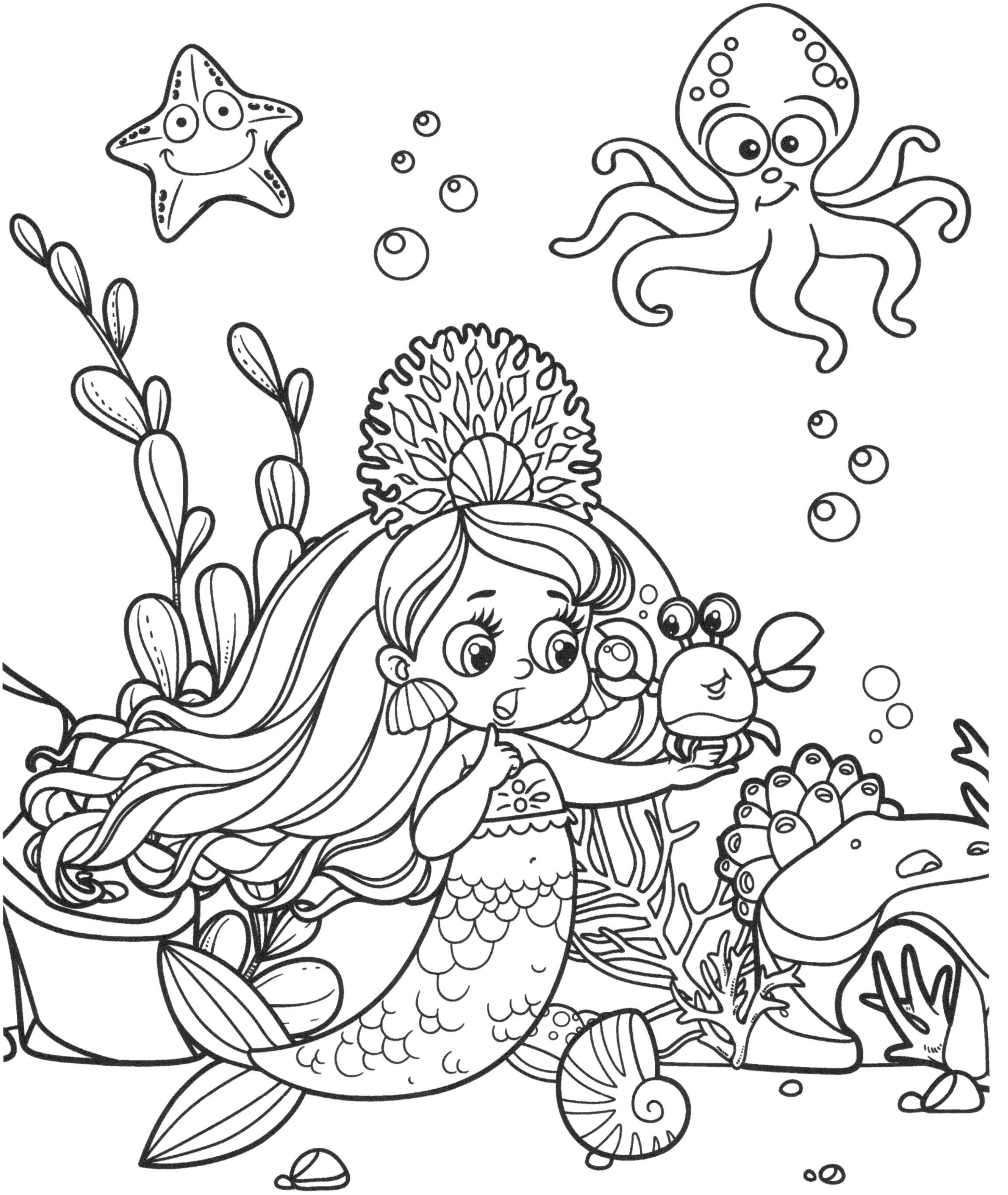

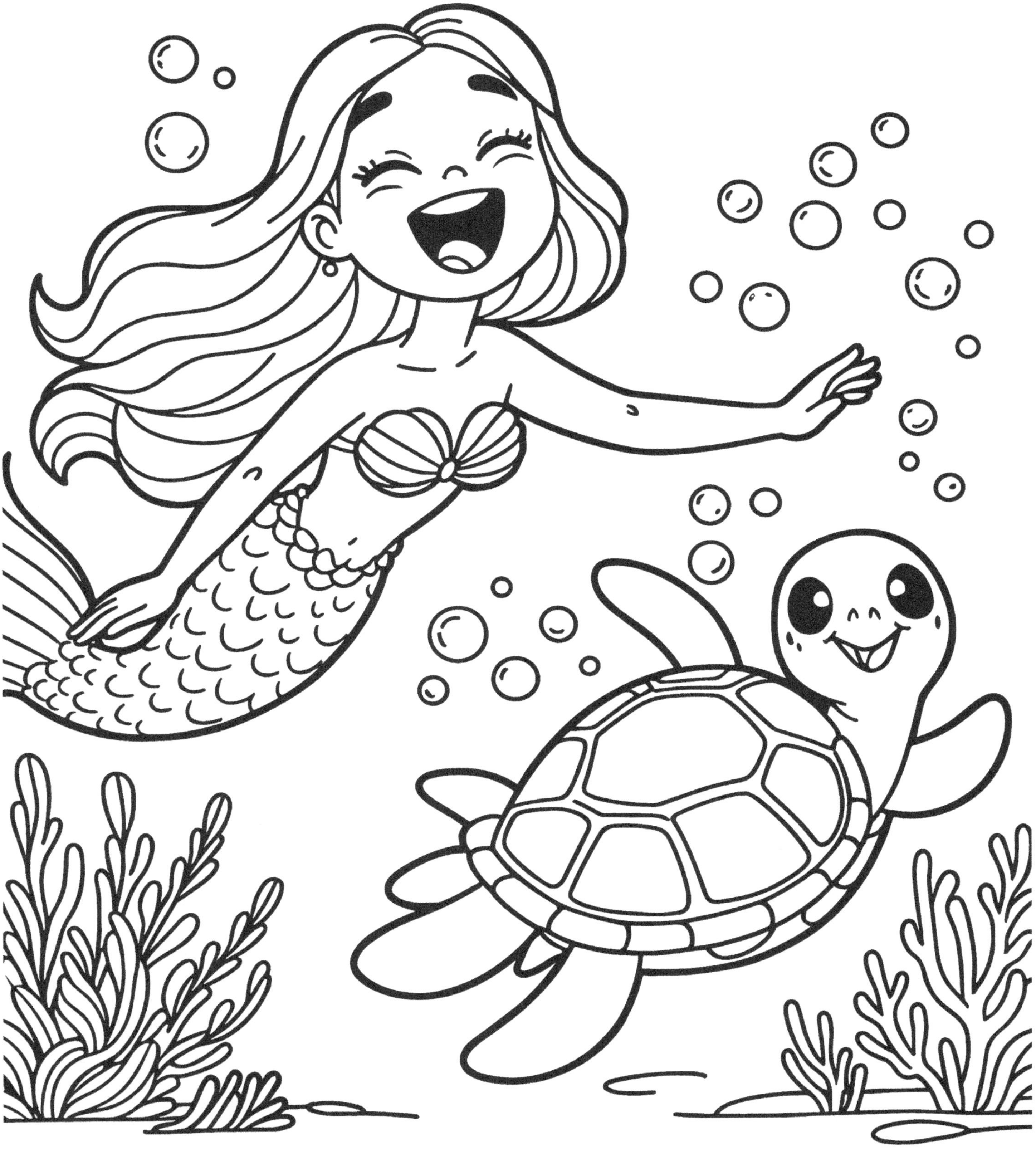

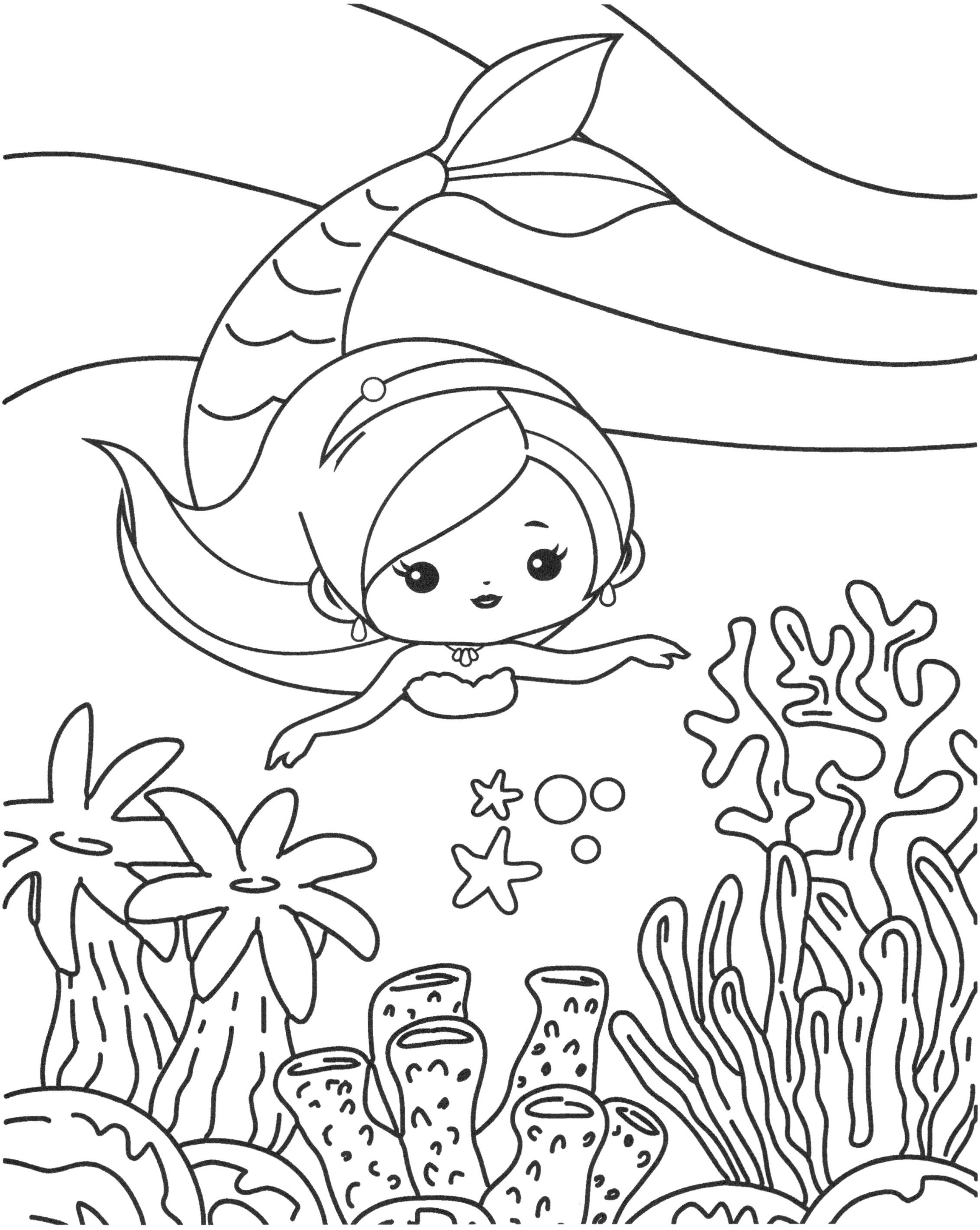

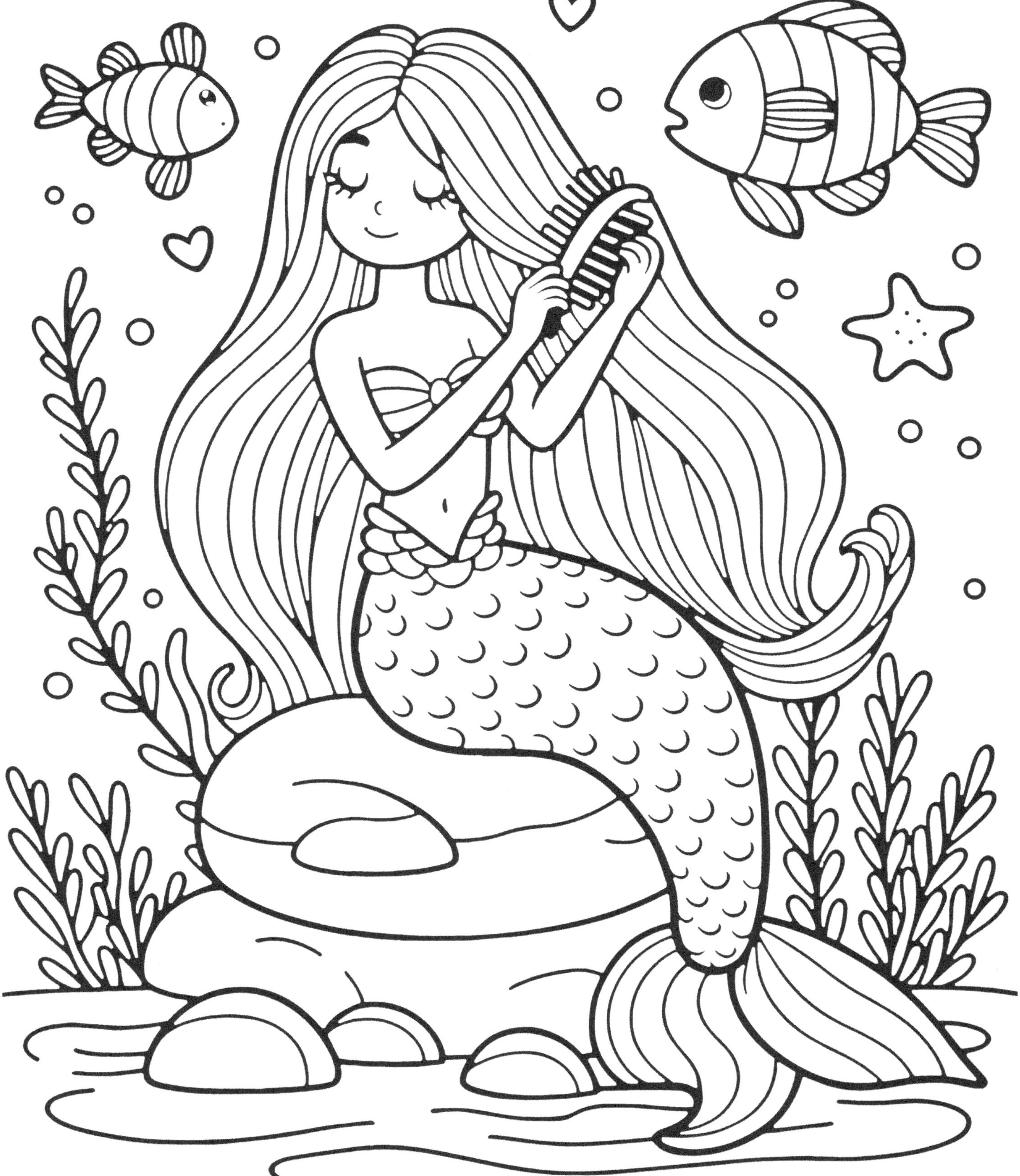

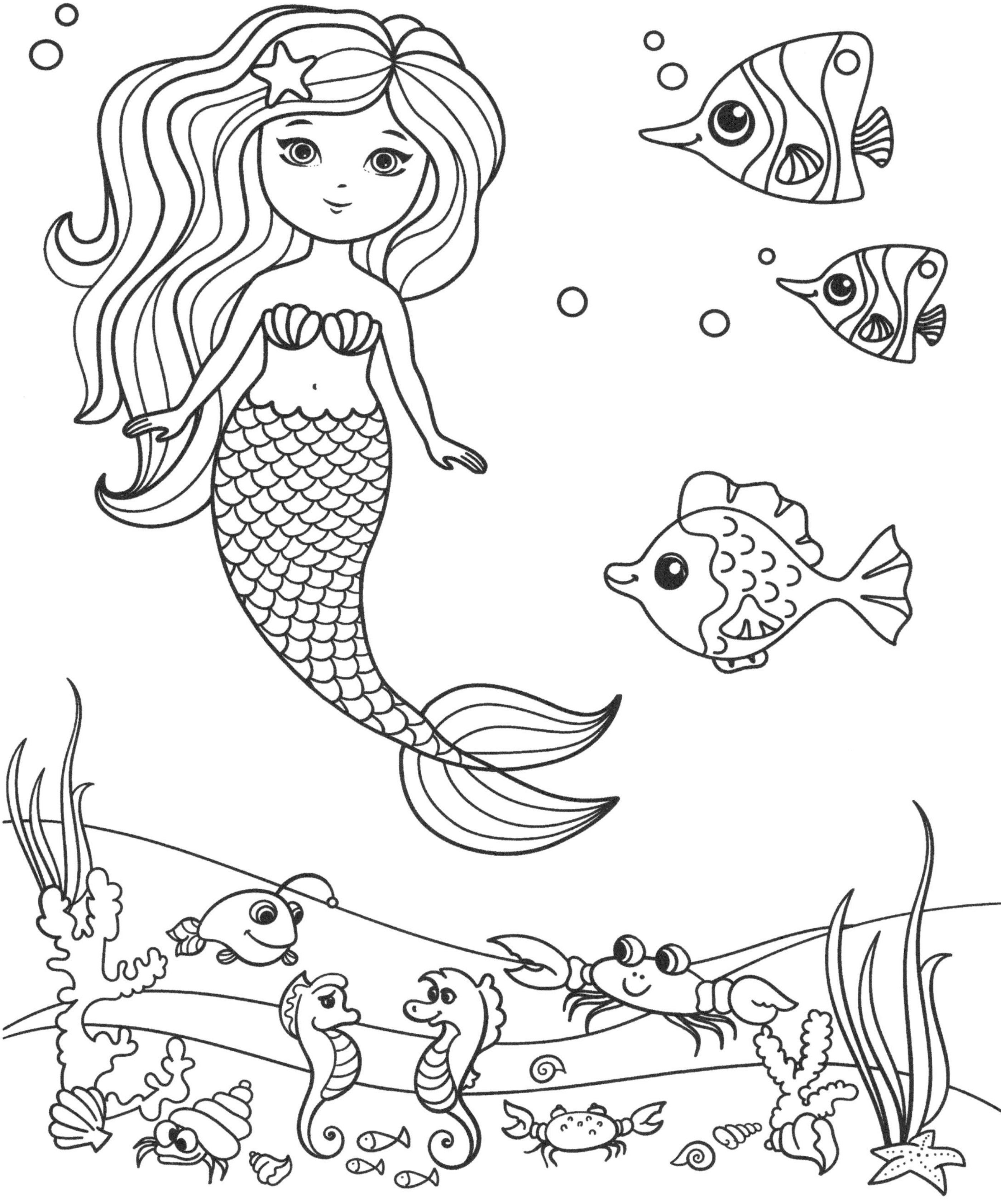

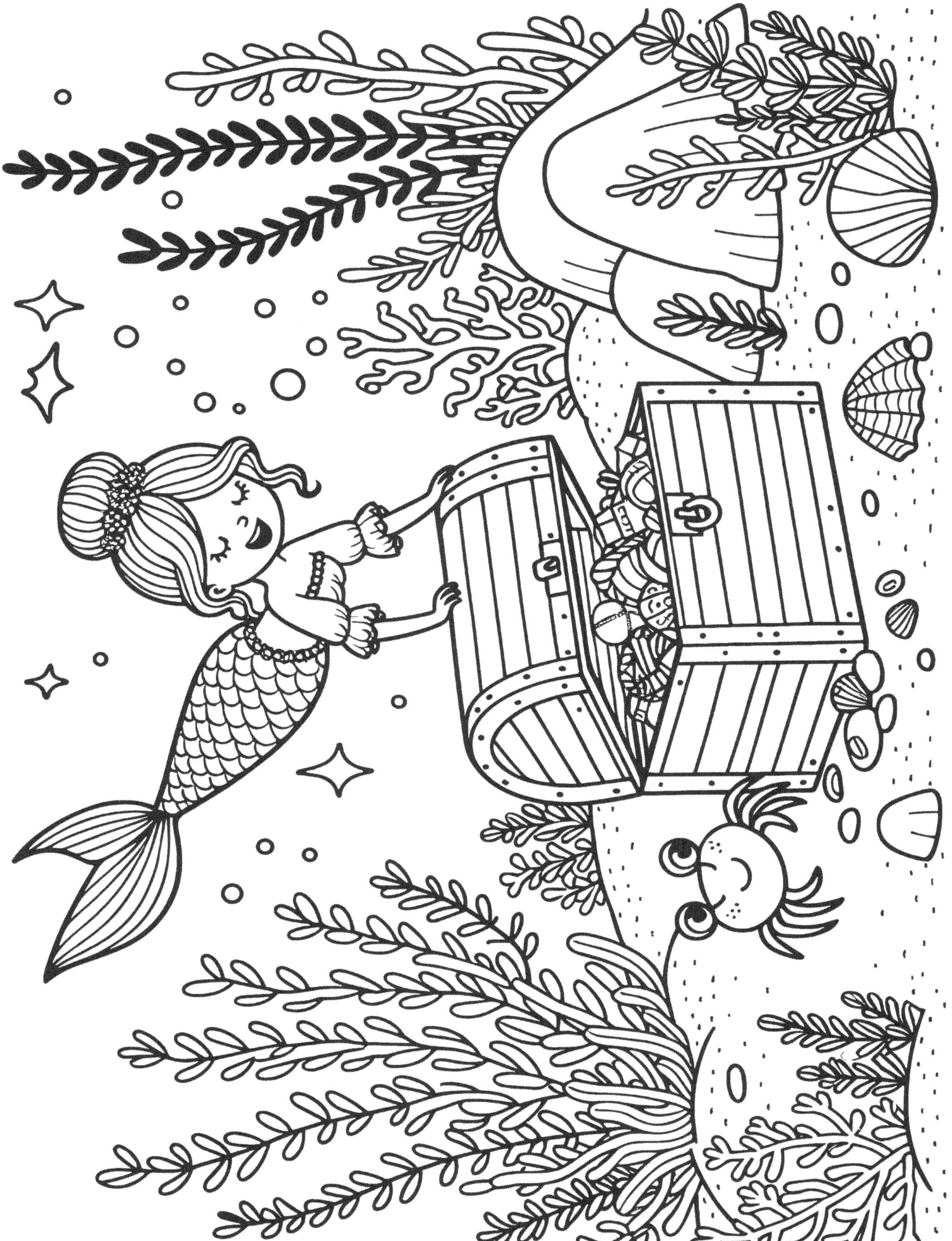

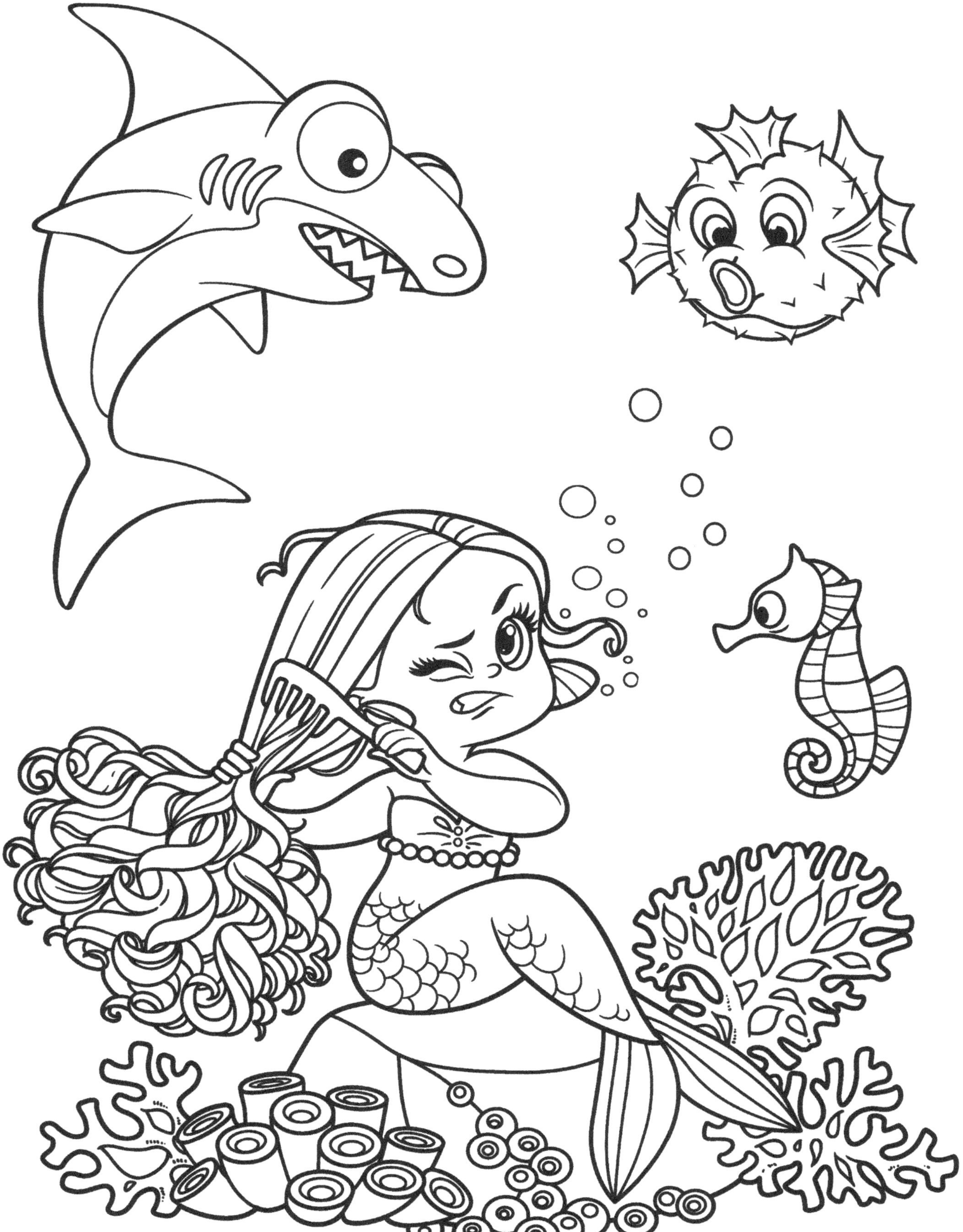

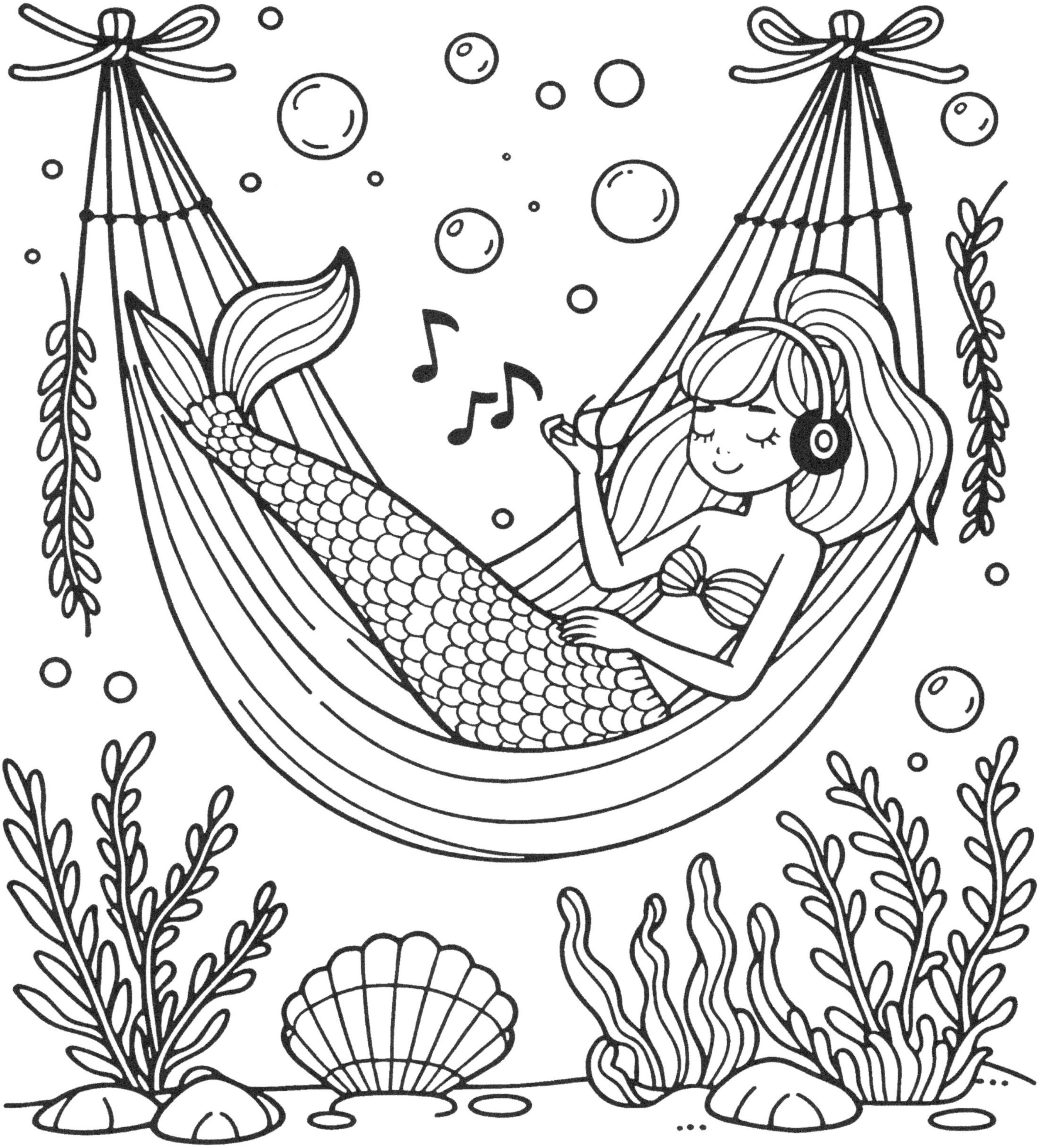

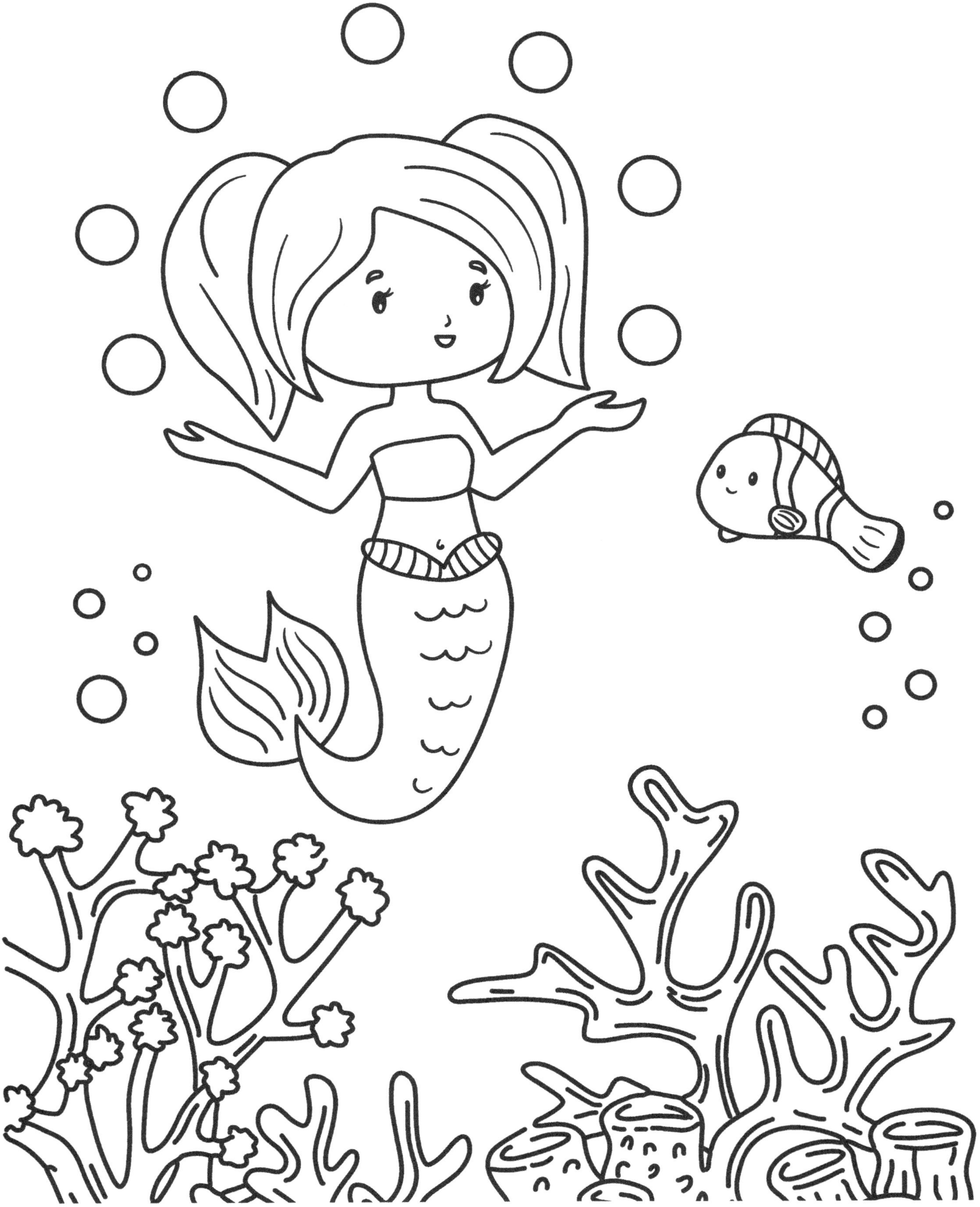

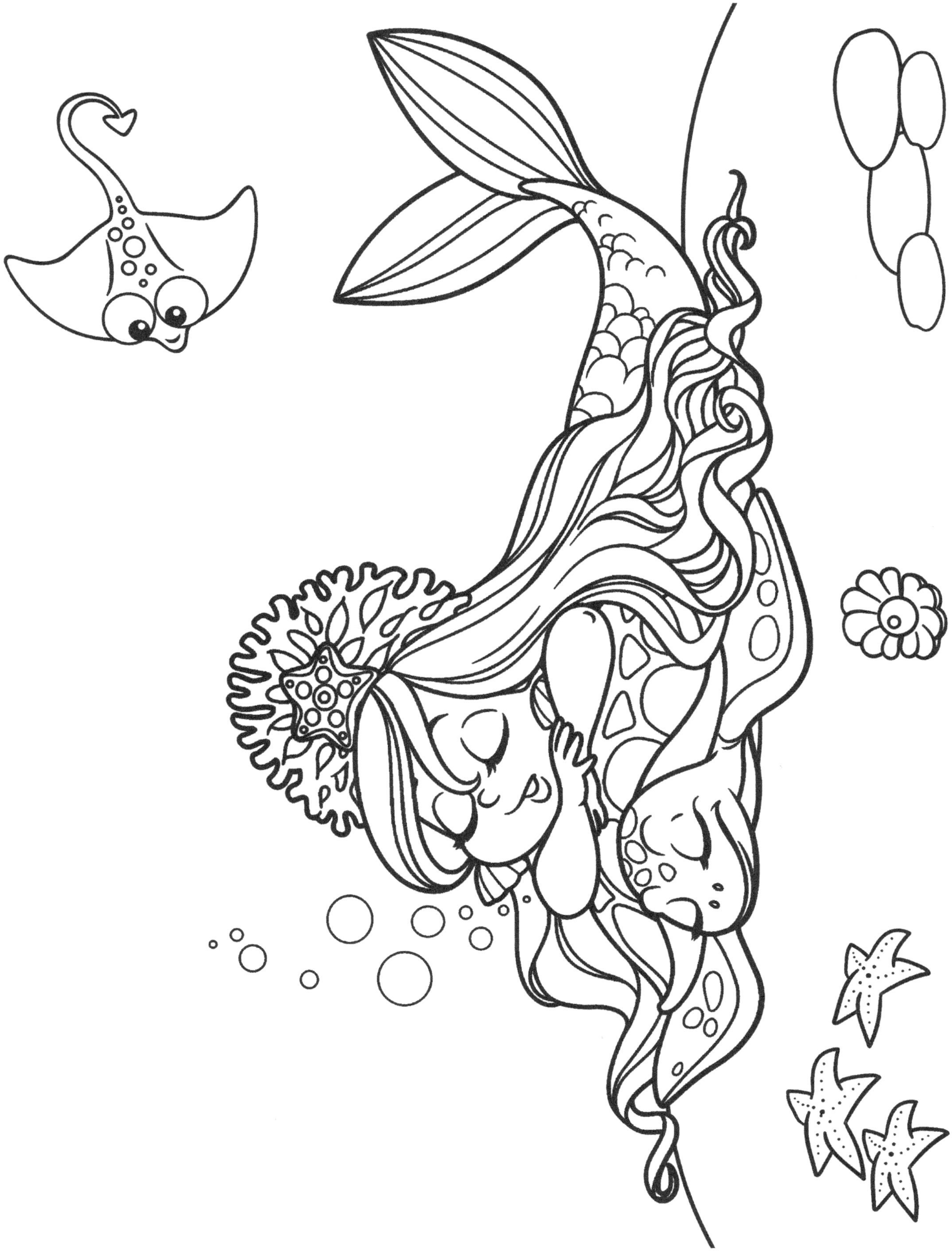

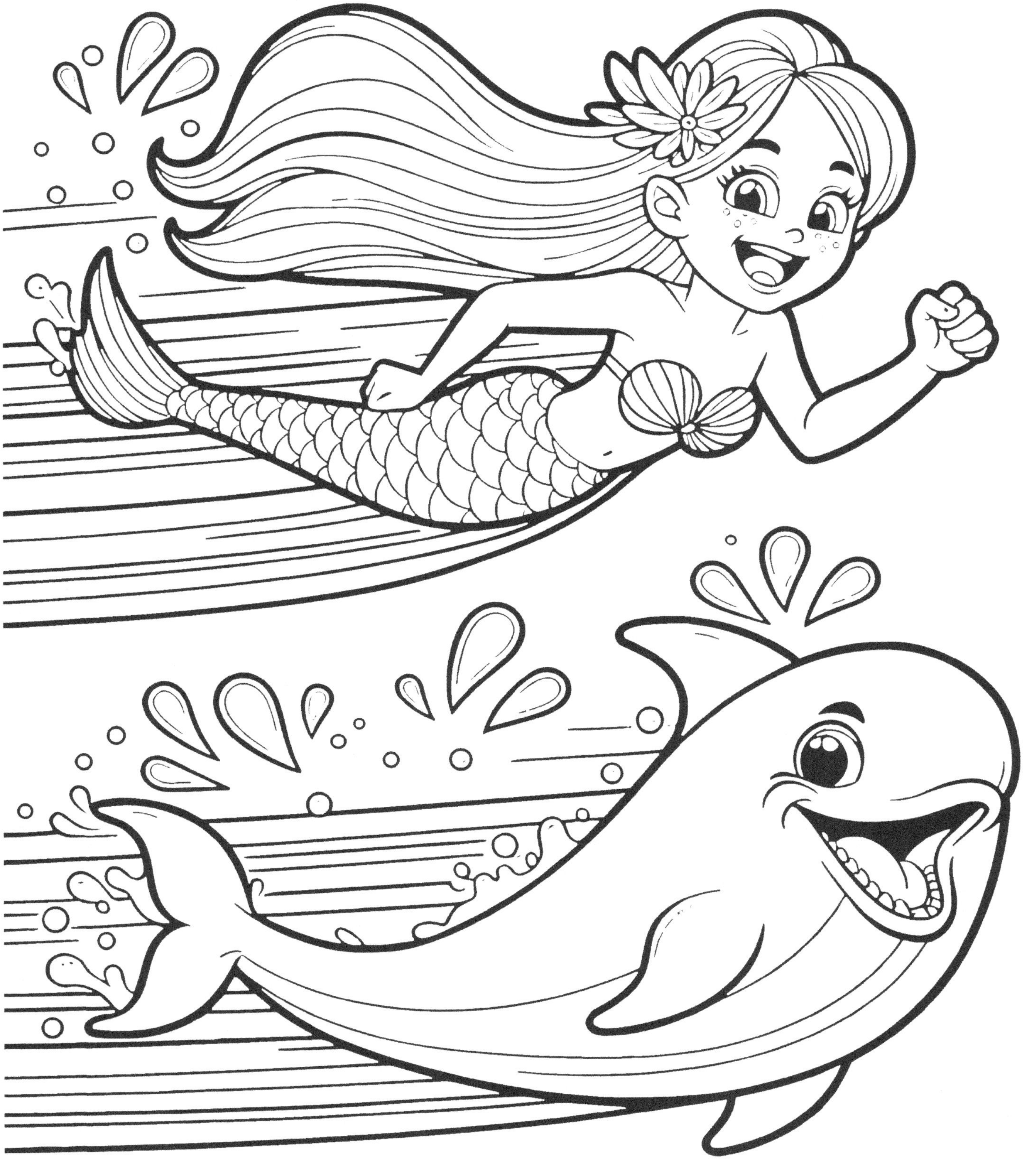

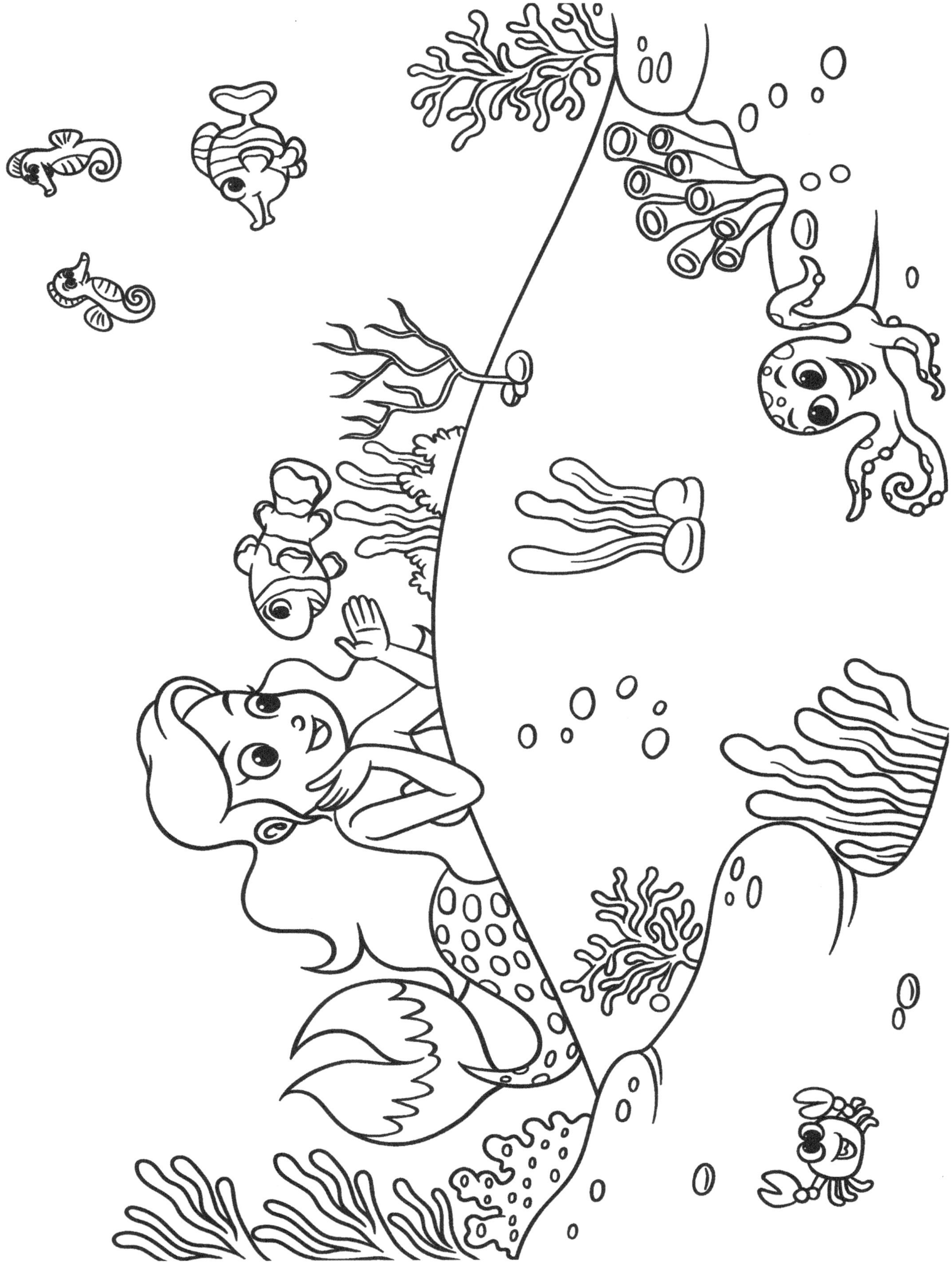

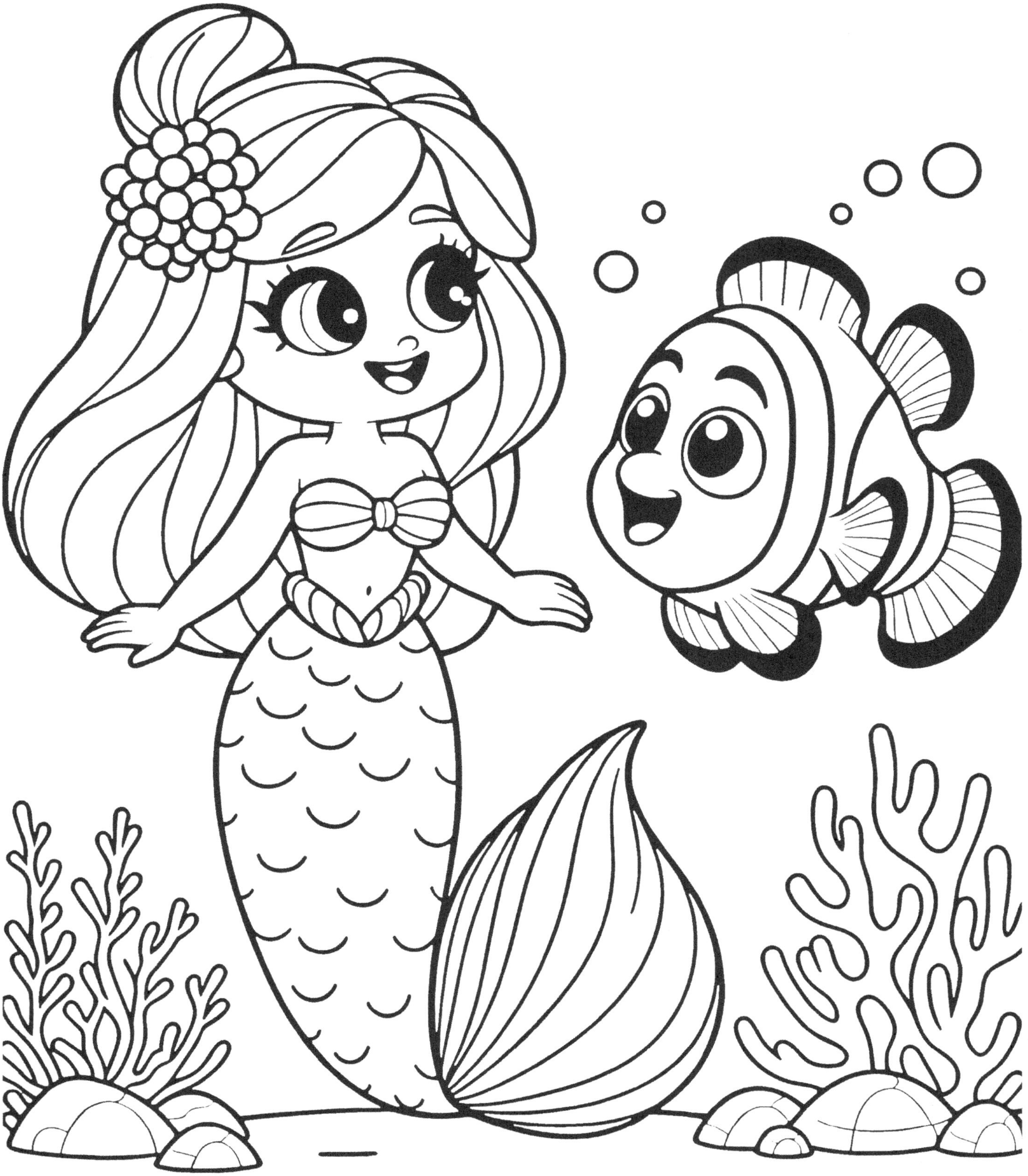

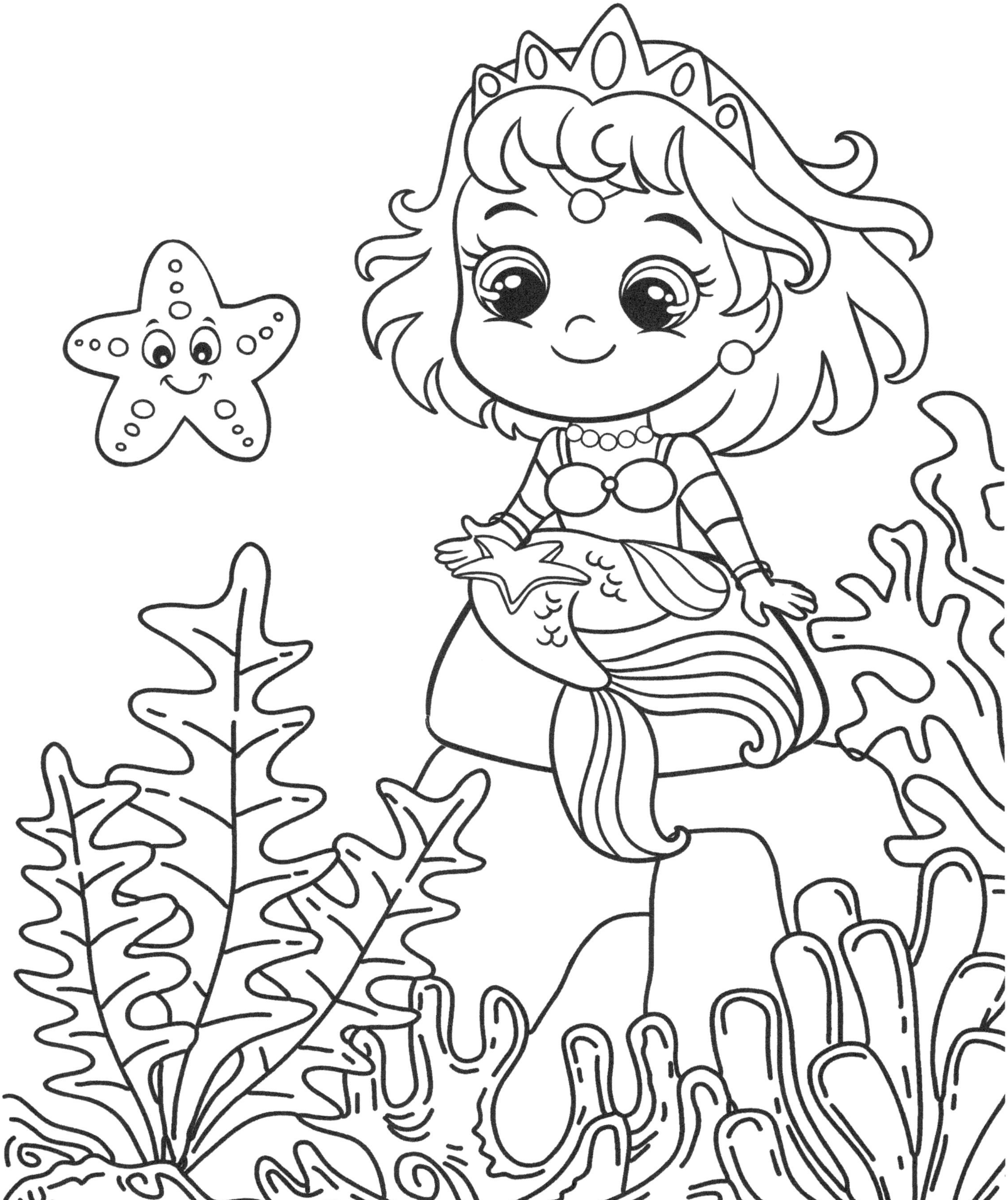

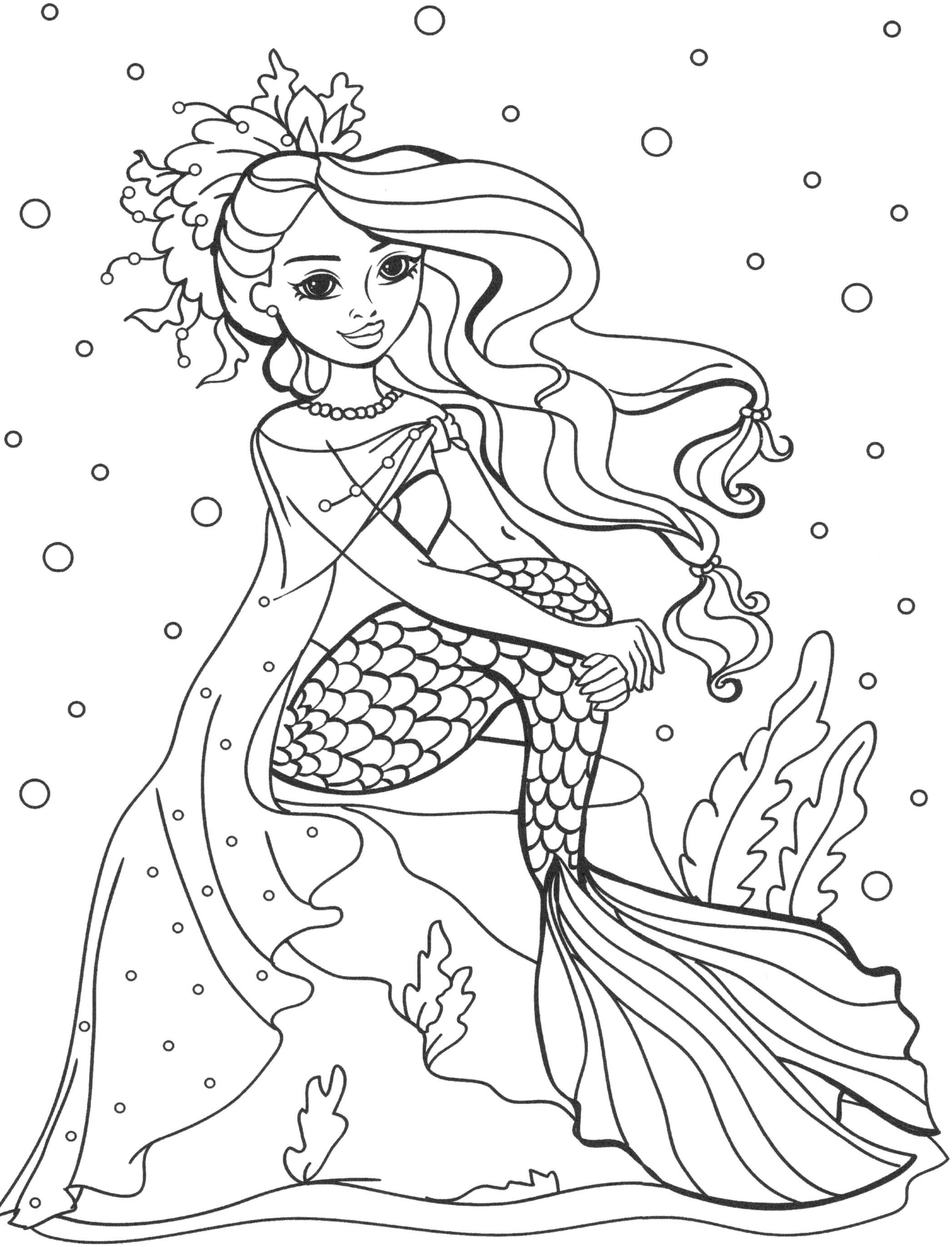

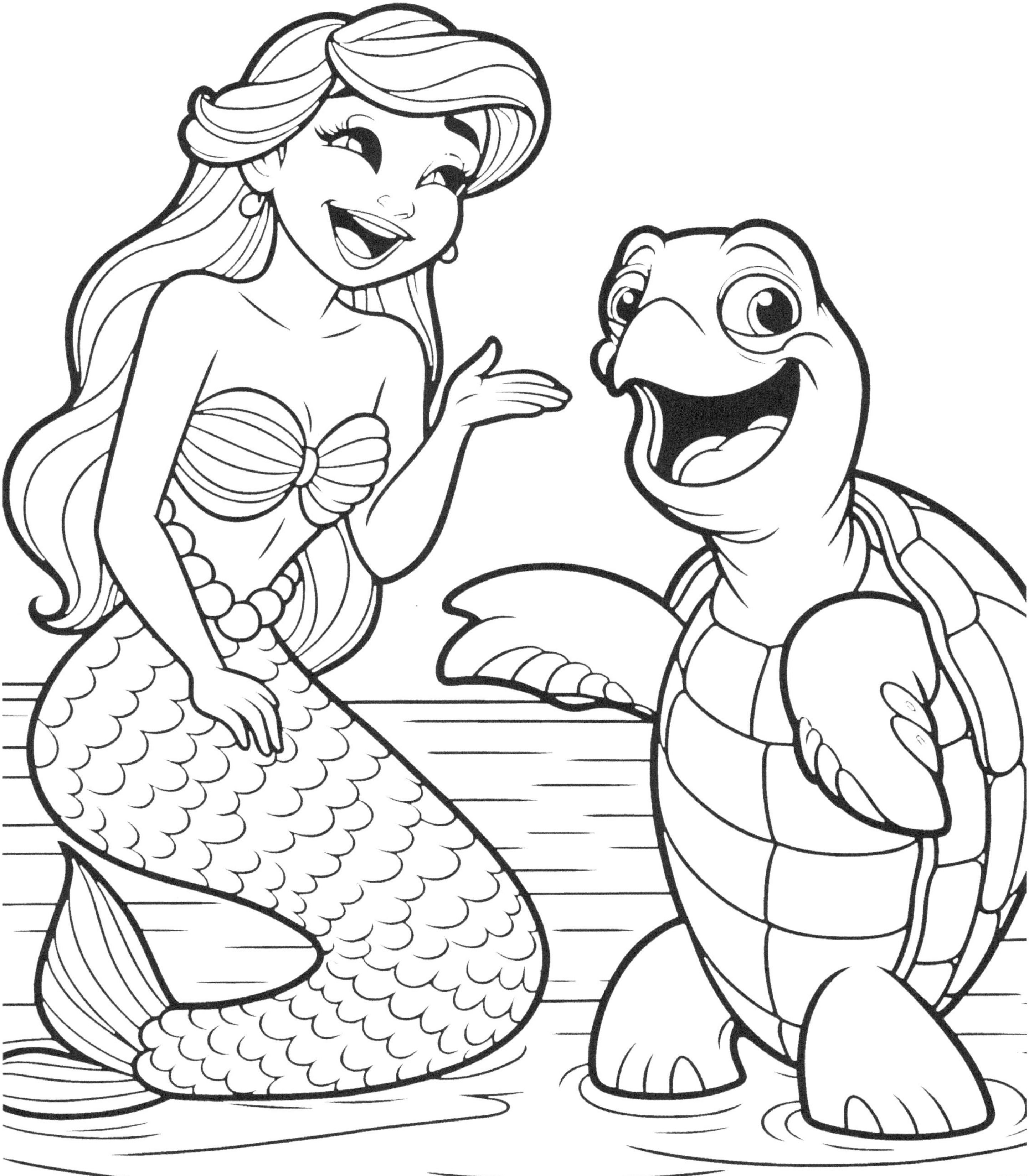

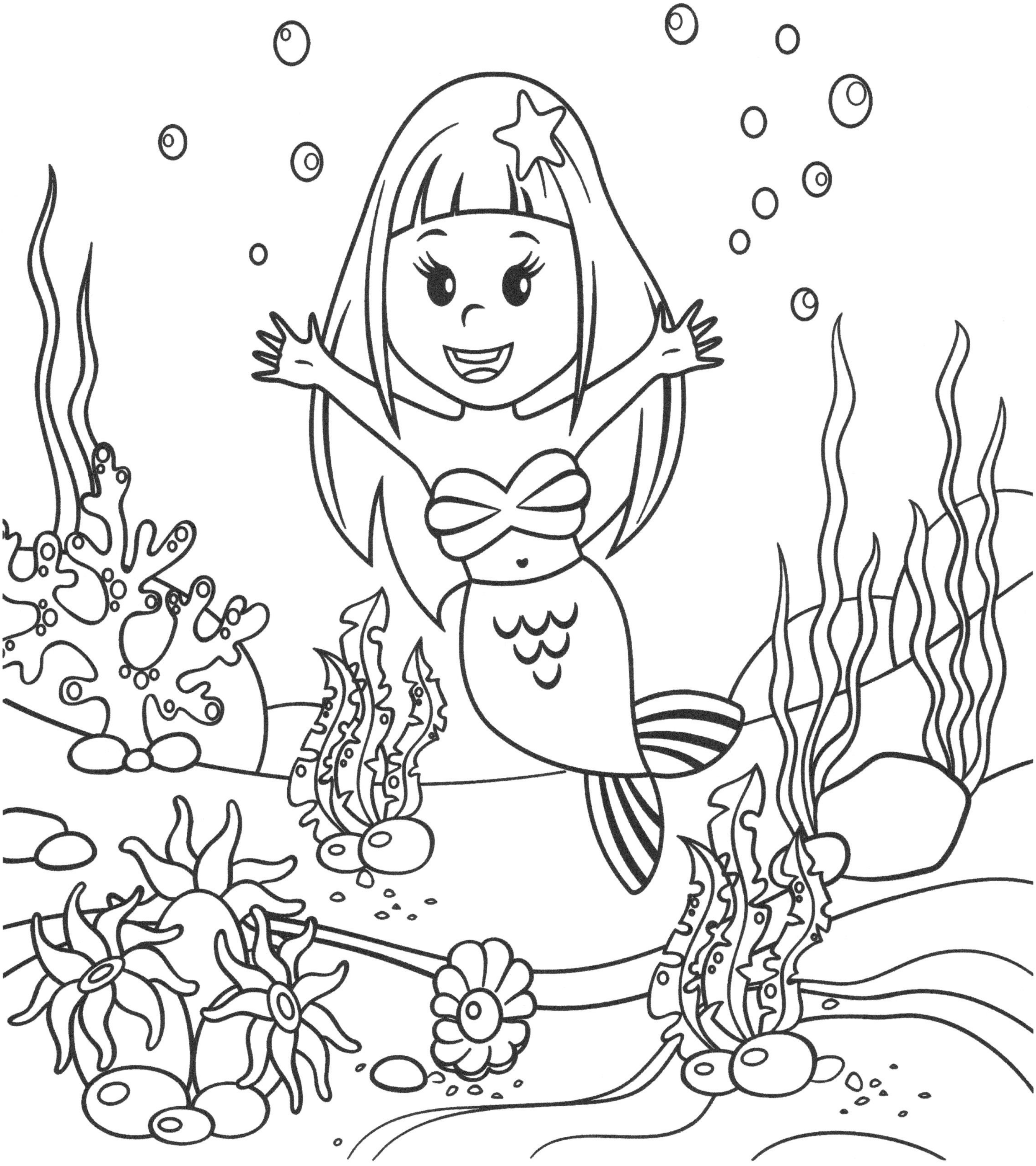

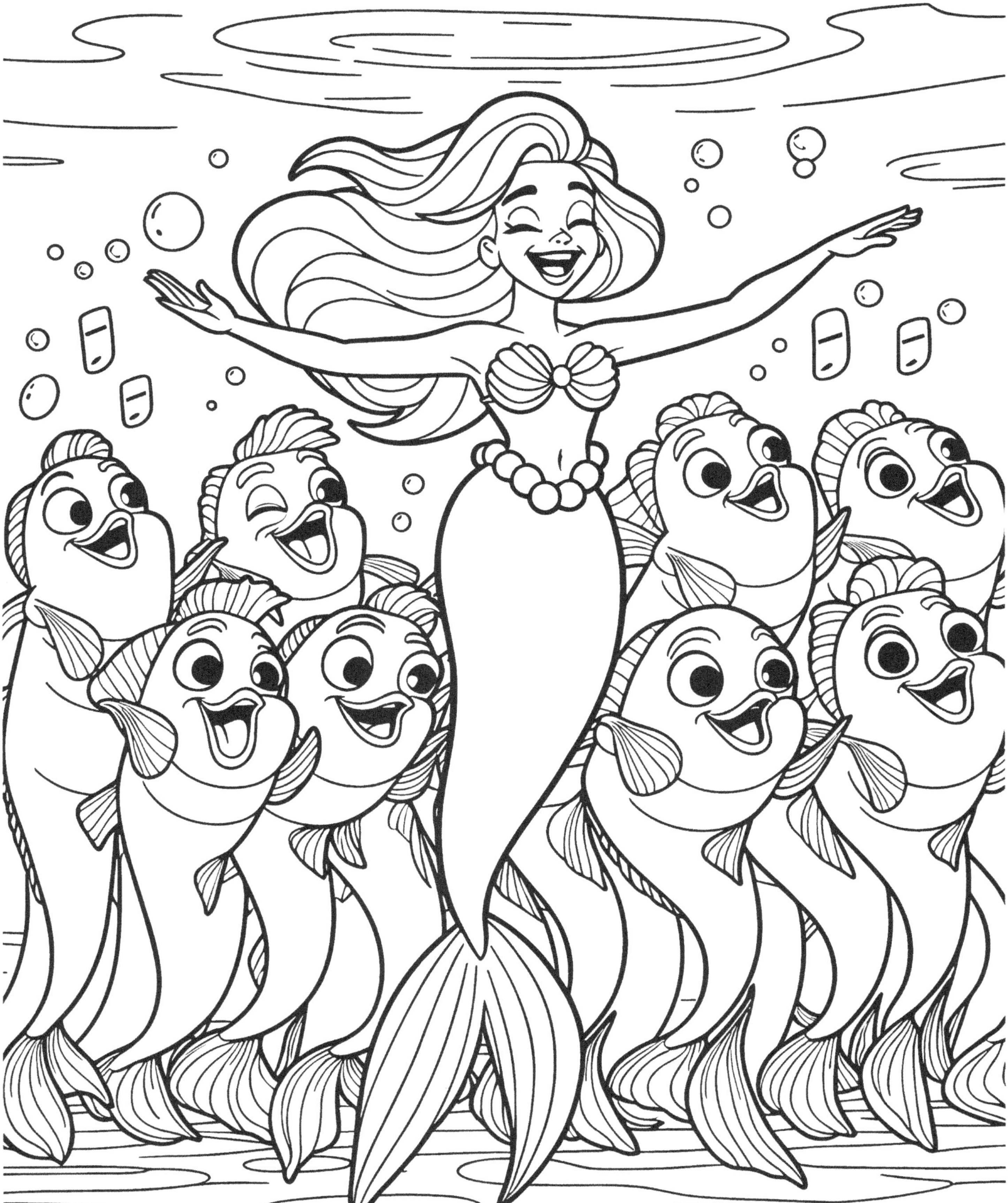

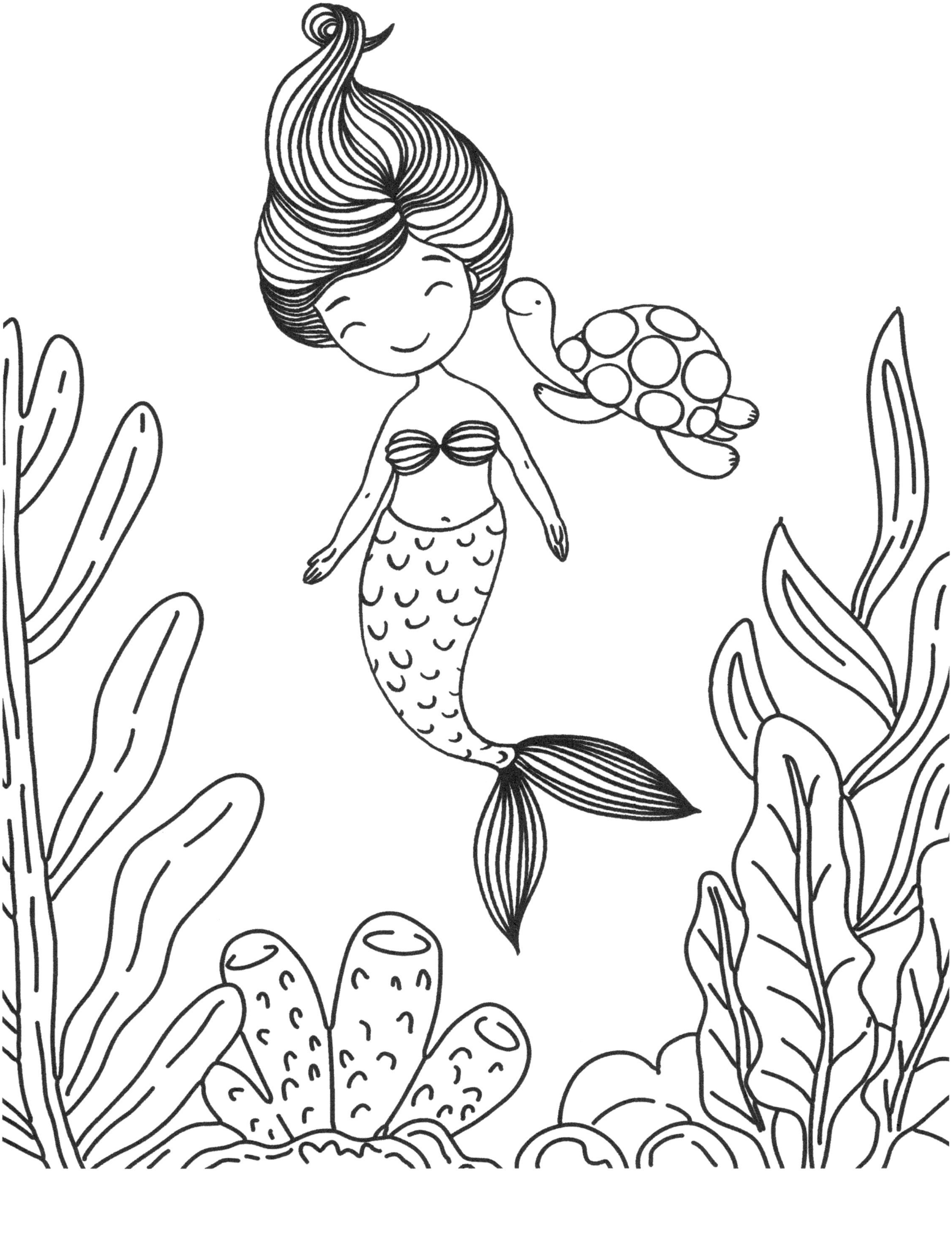

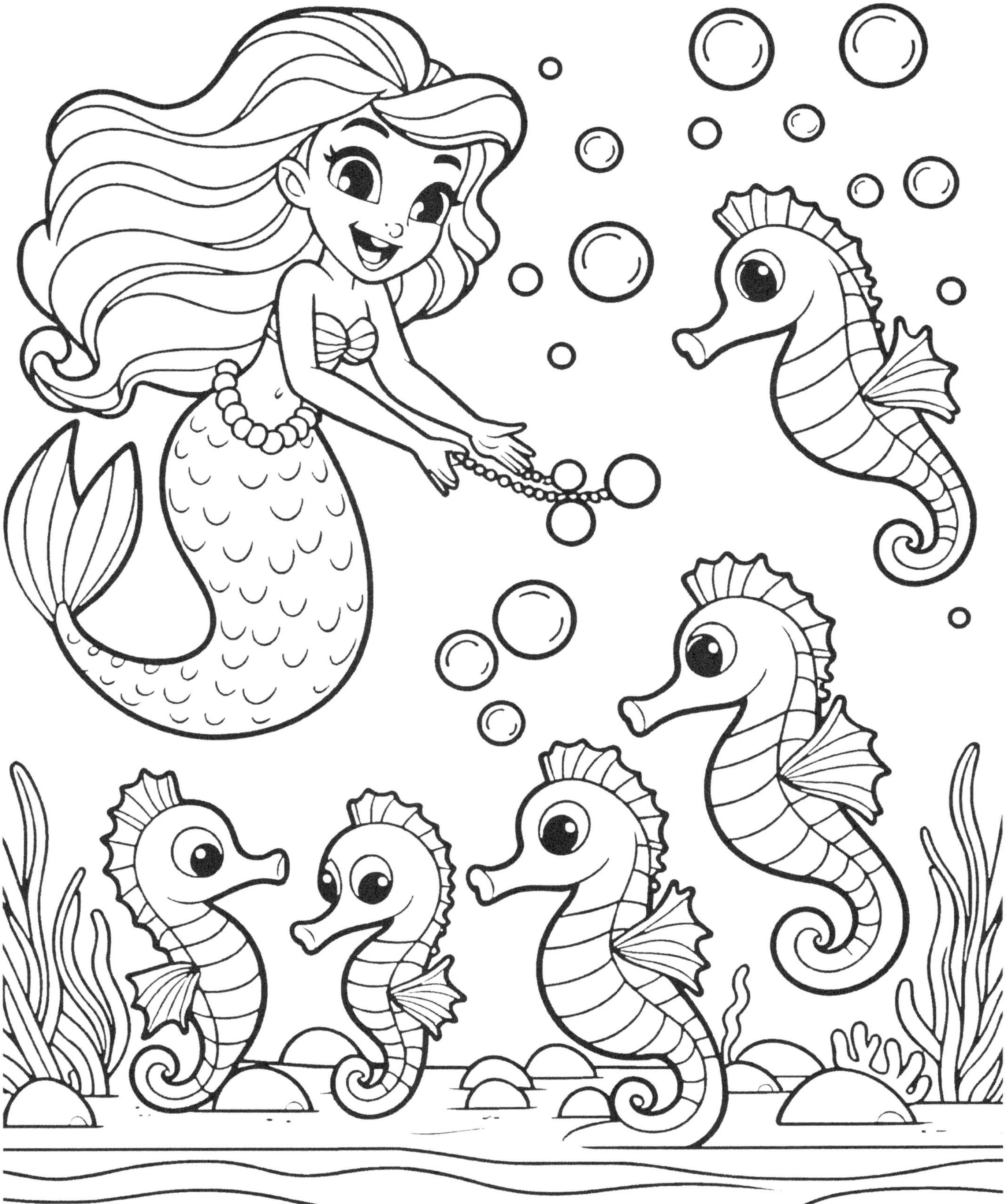

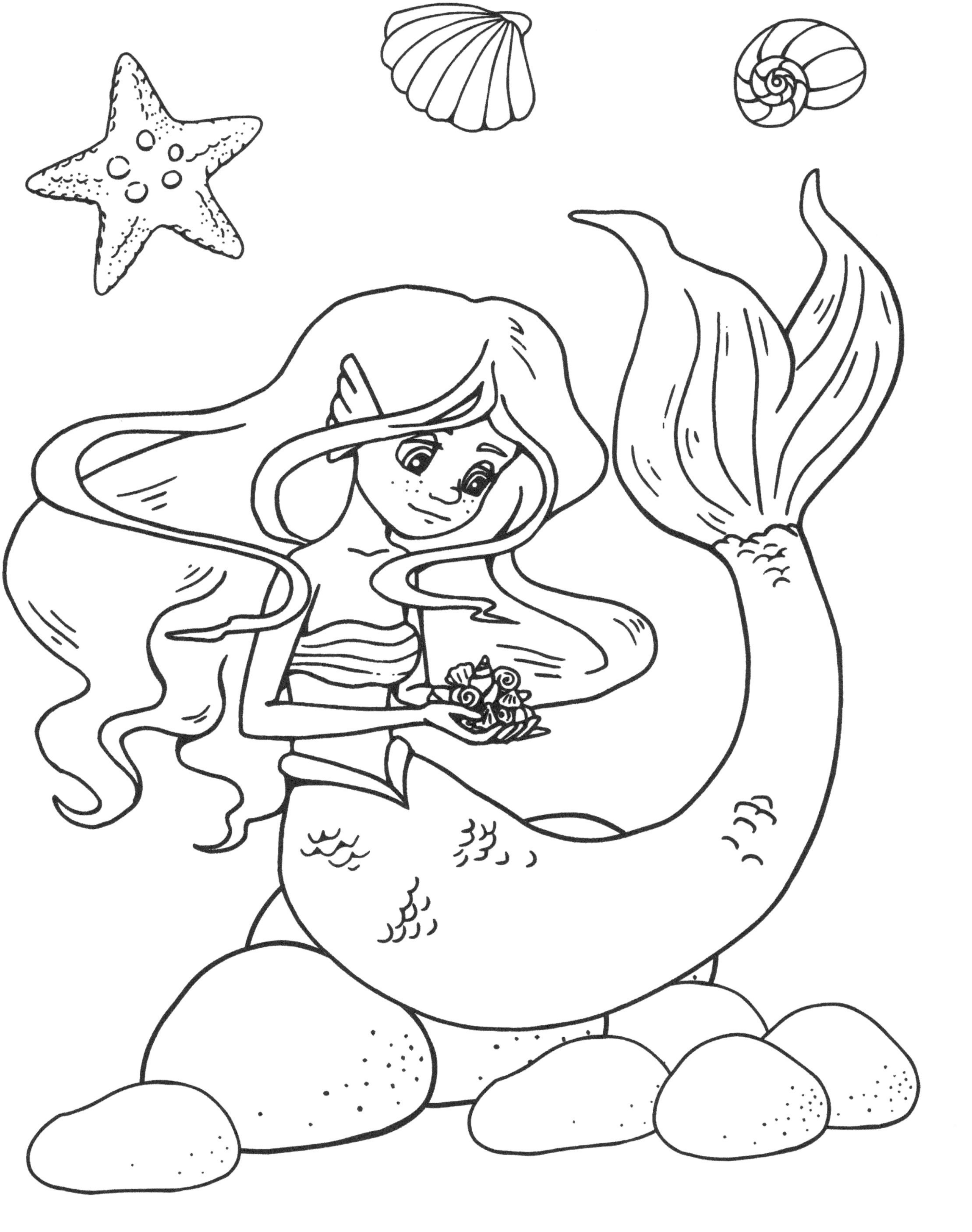

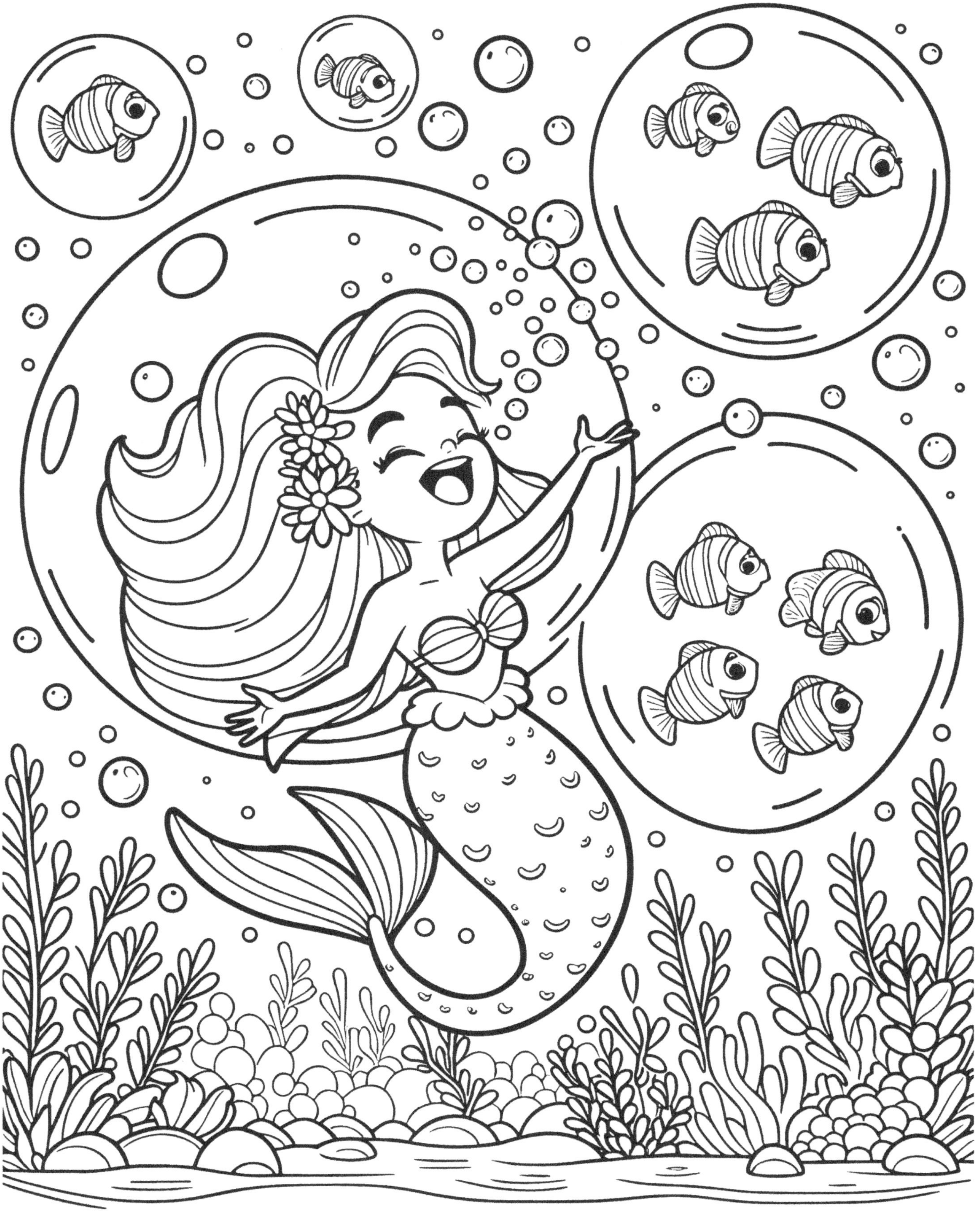

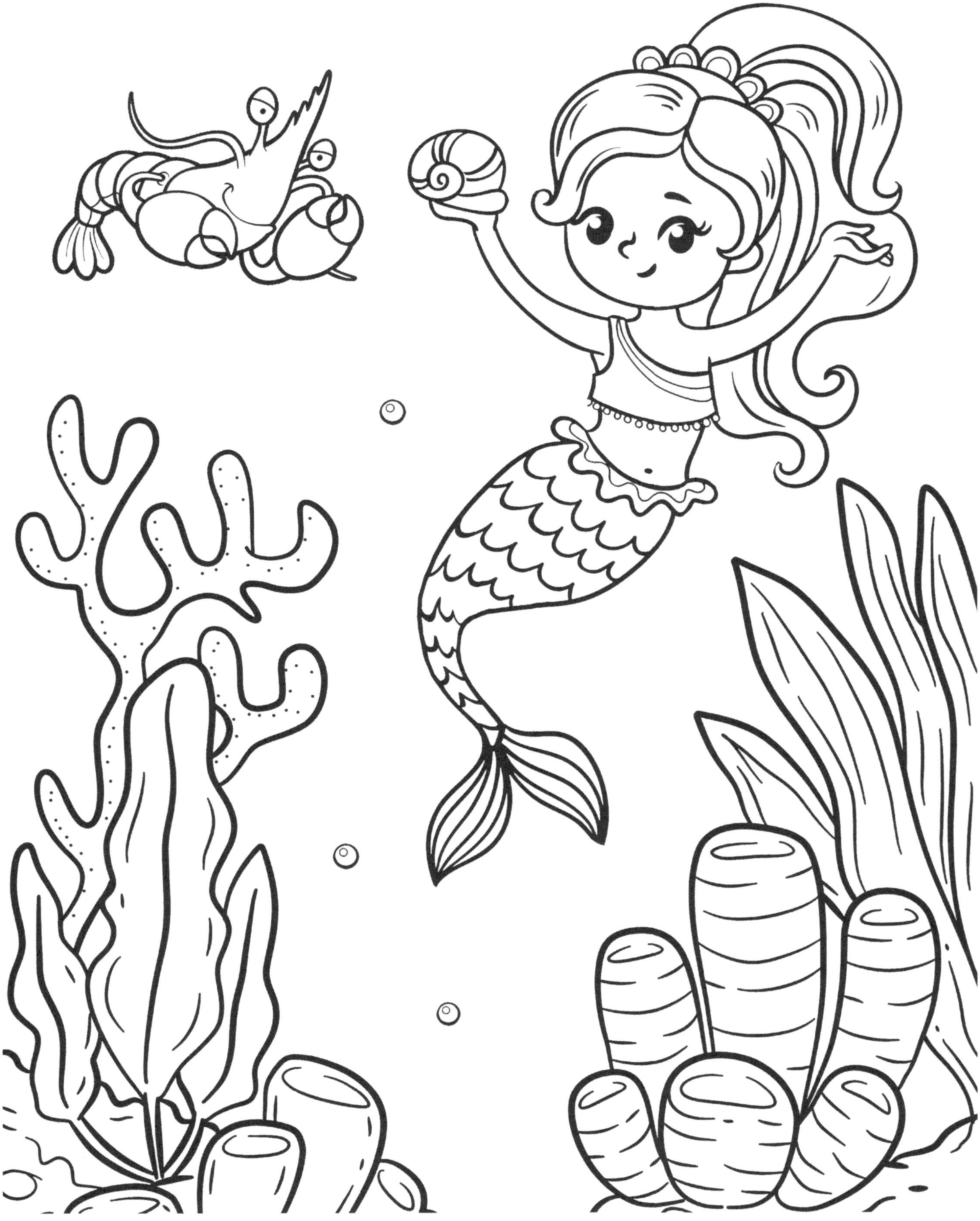

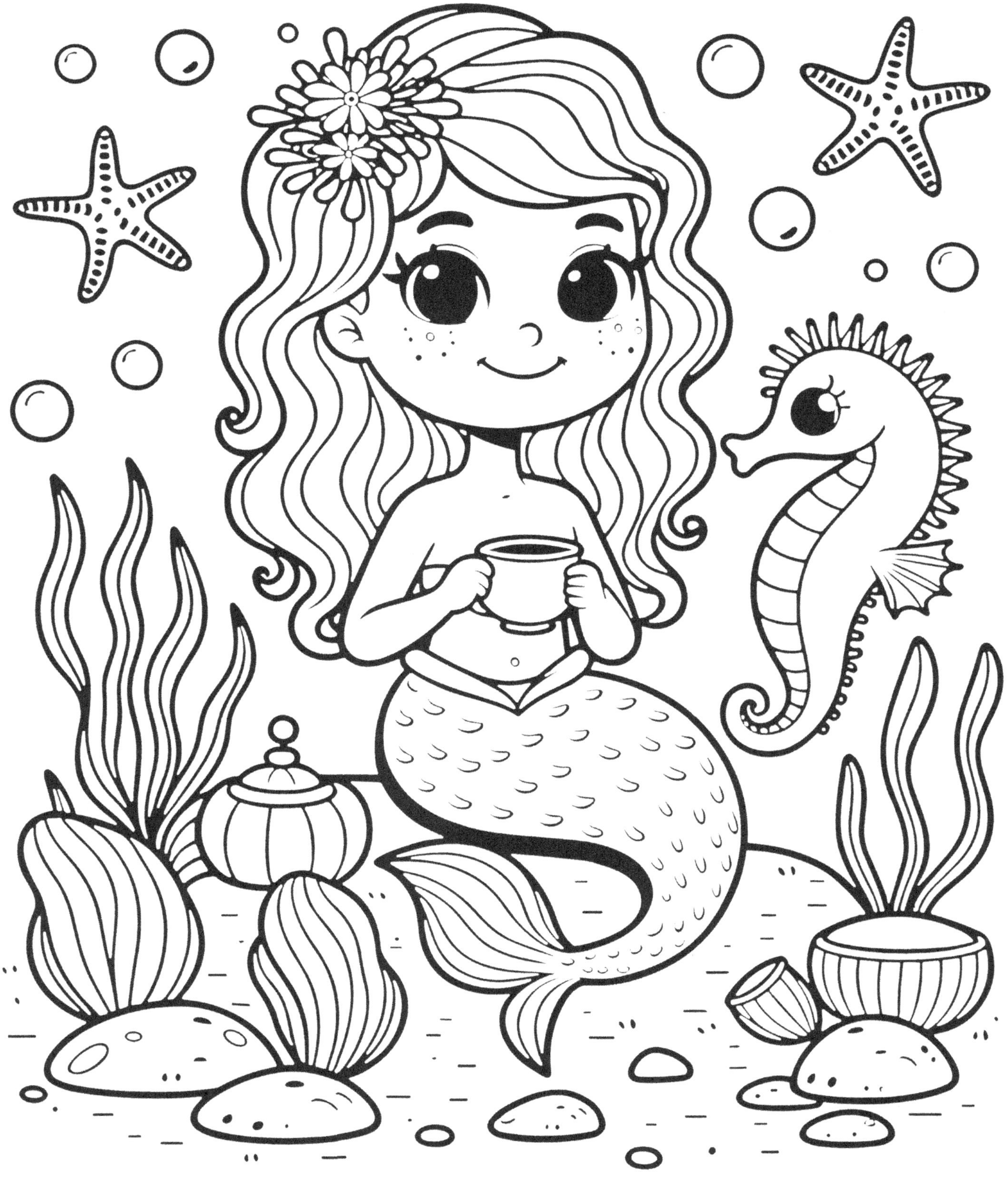

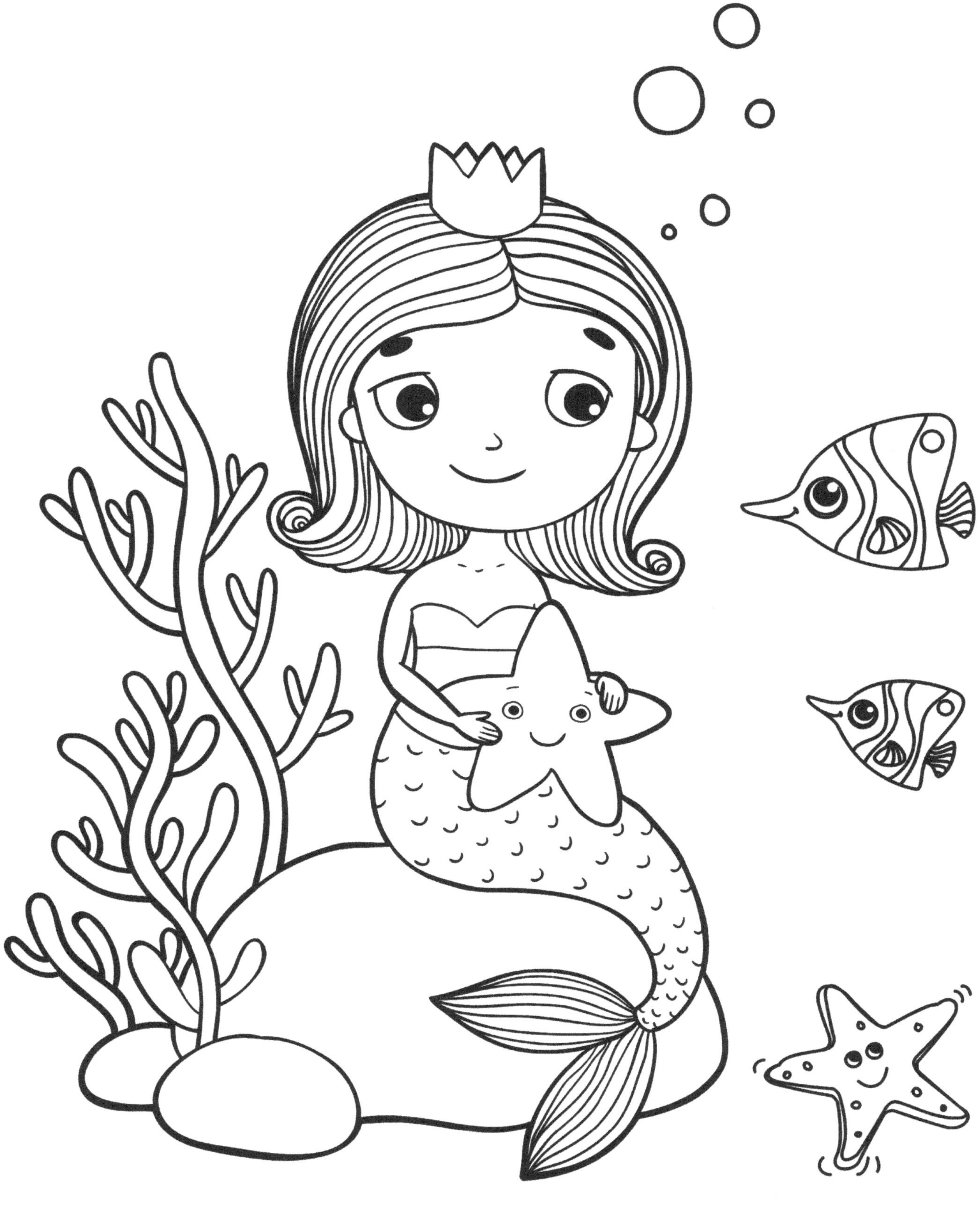

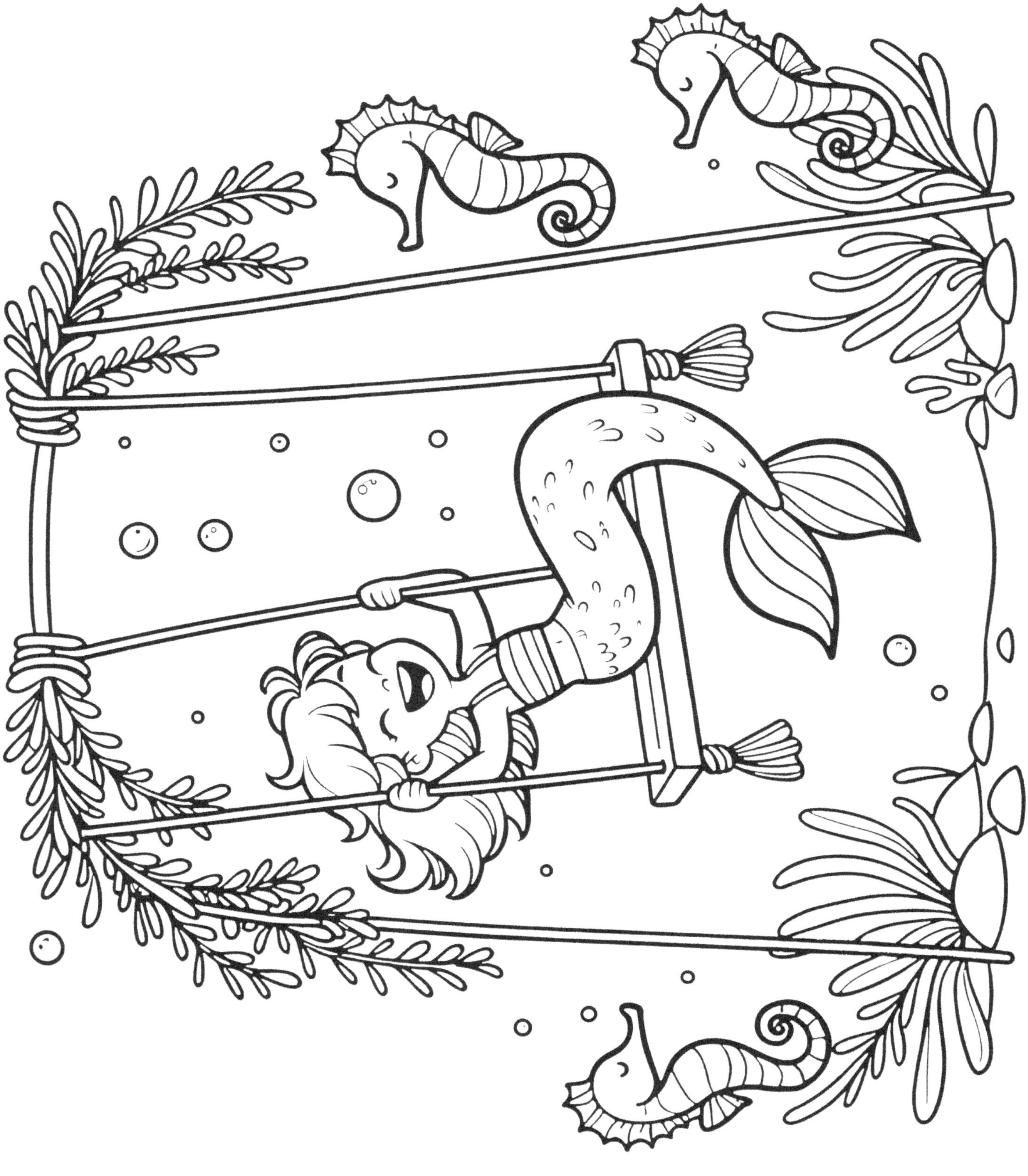

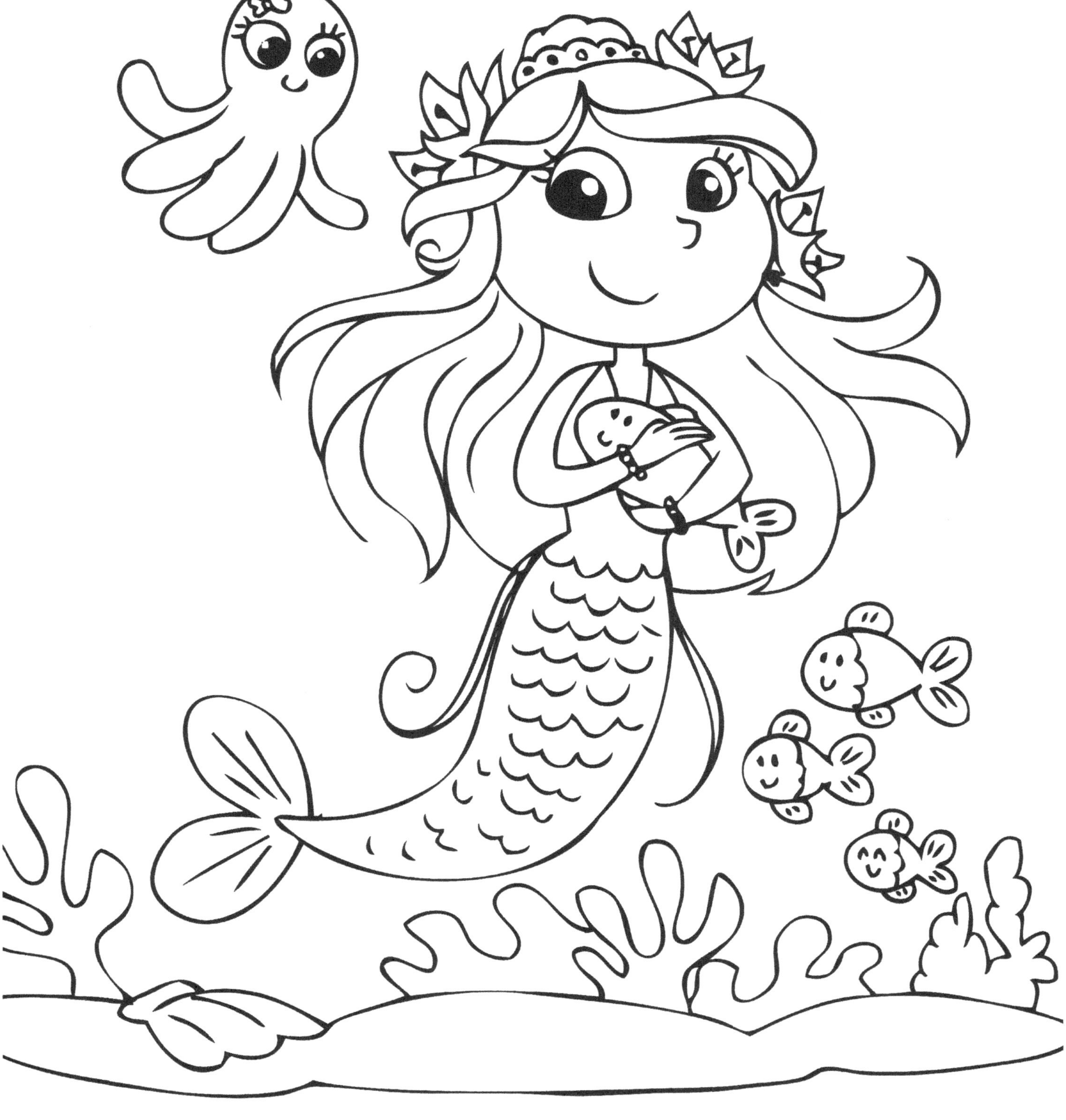

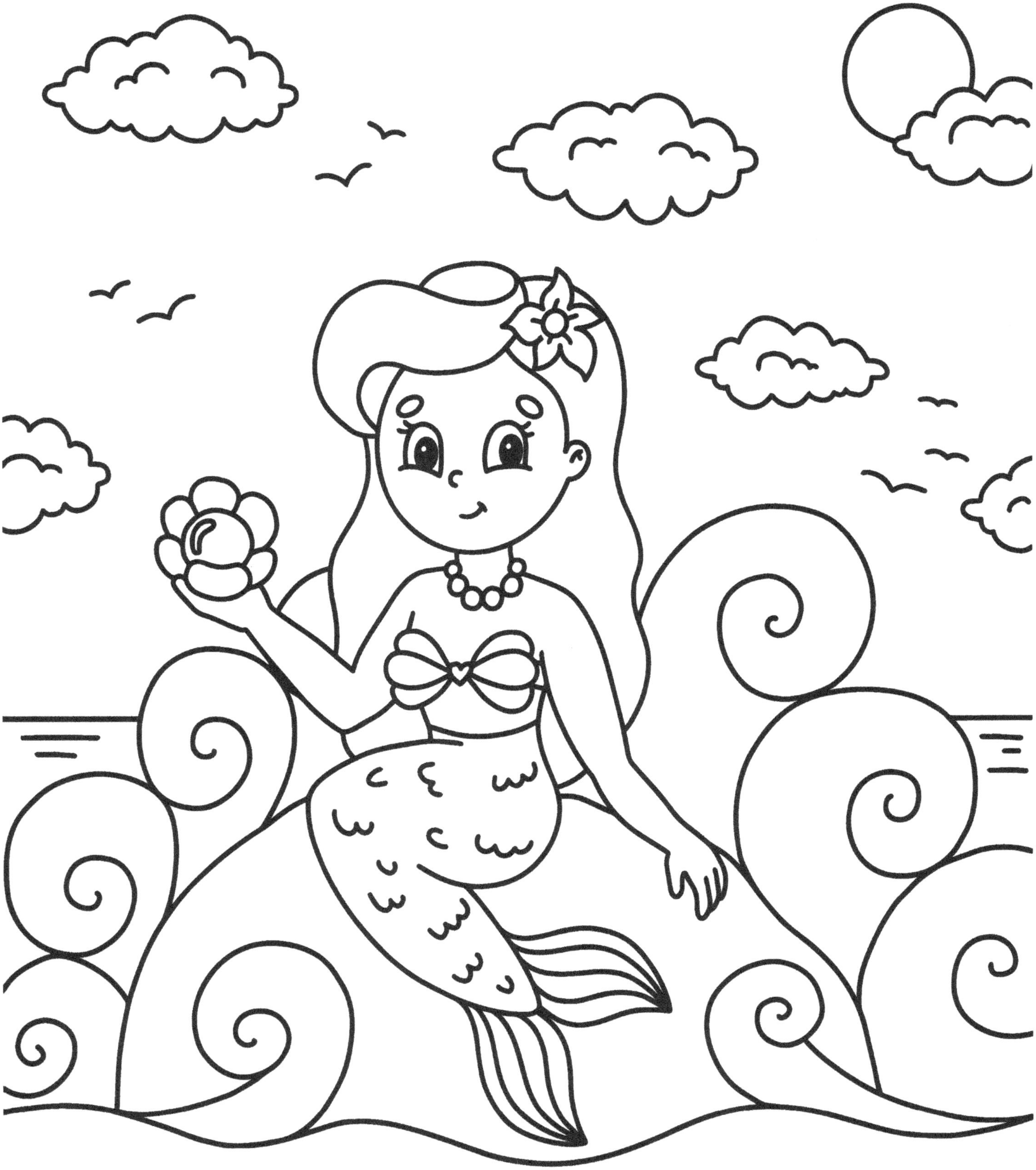

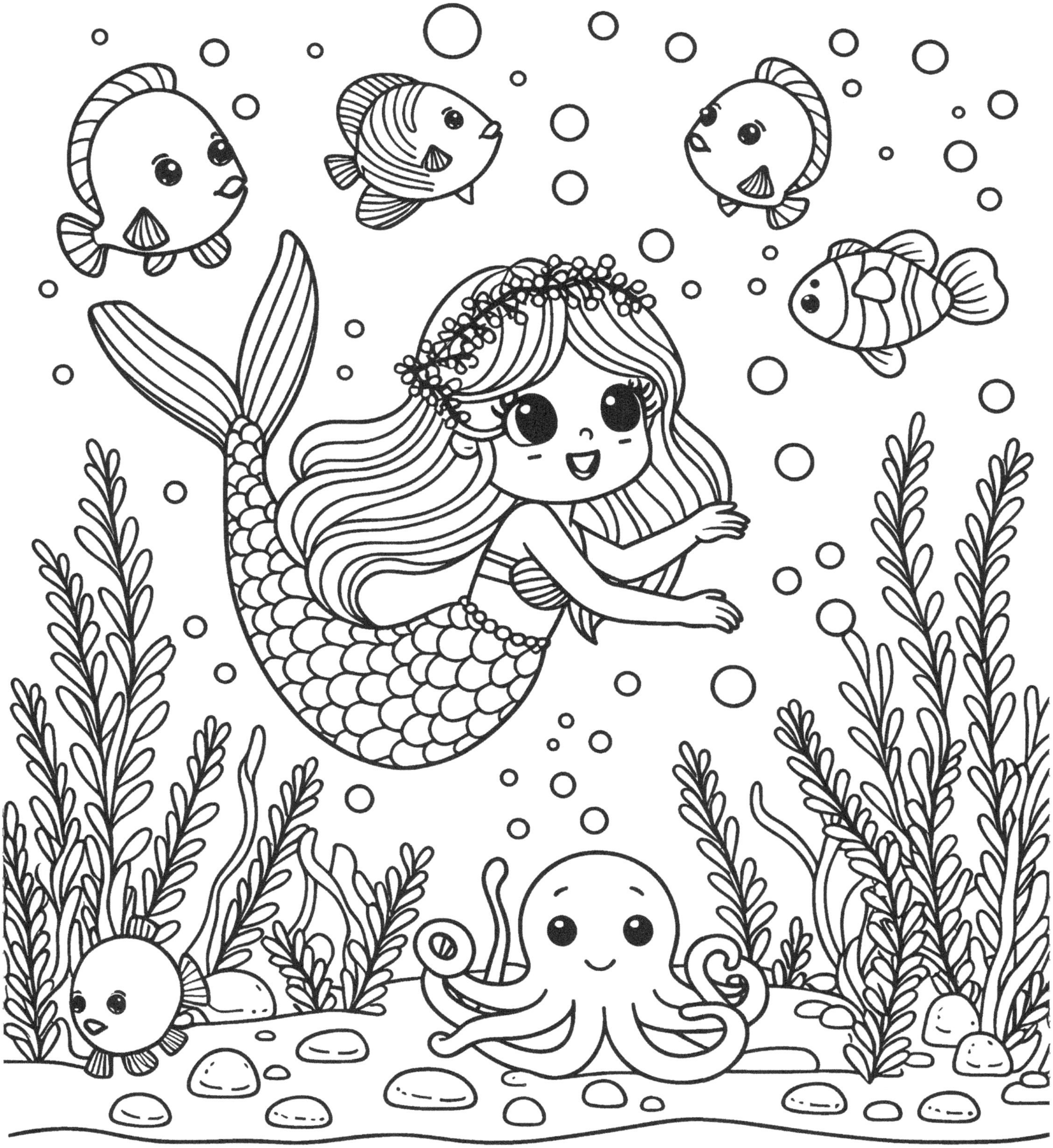

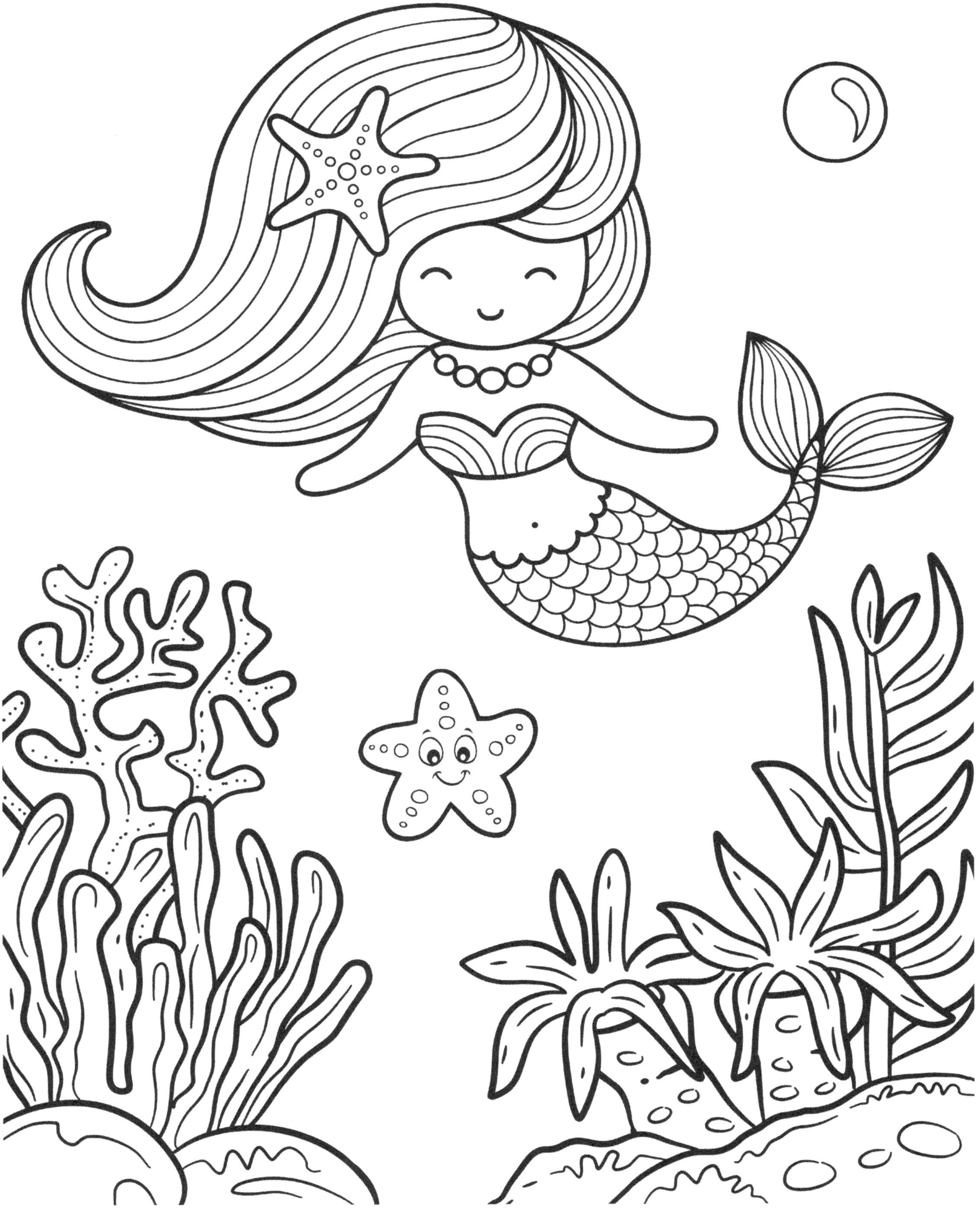

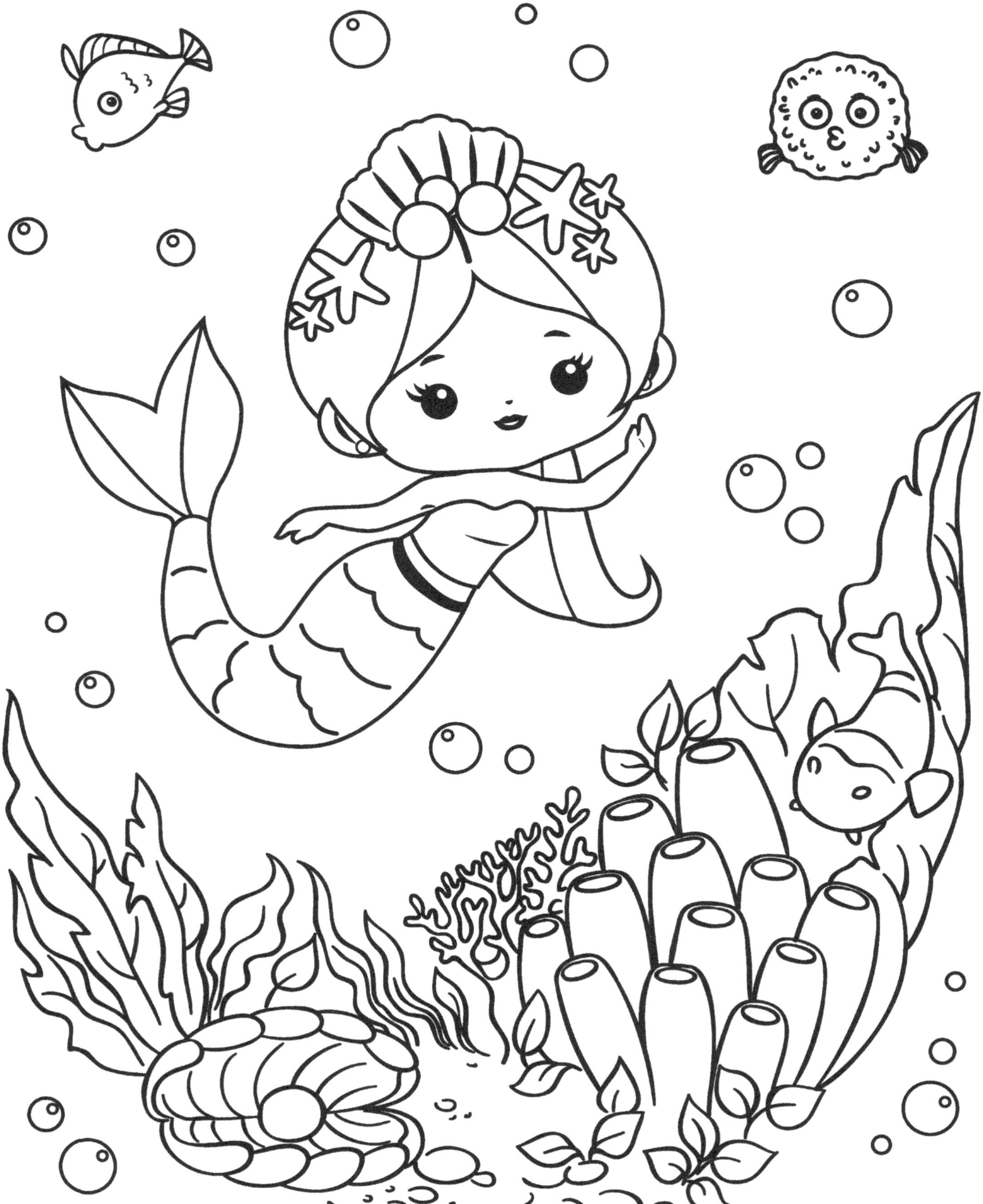

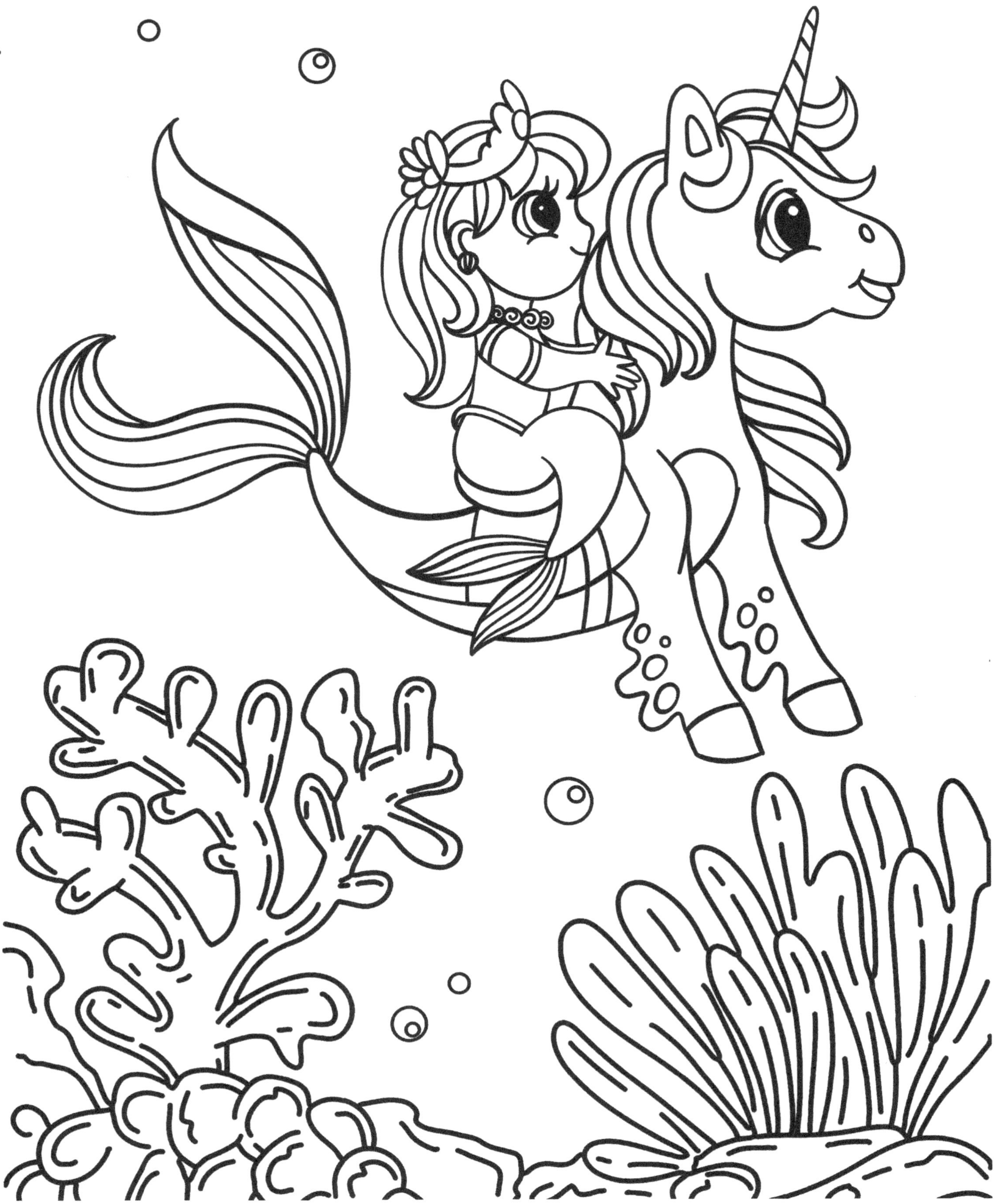

Also available from Golden Age Press...

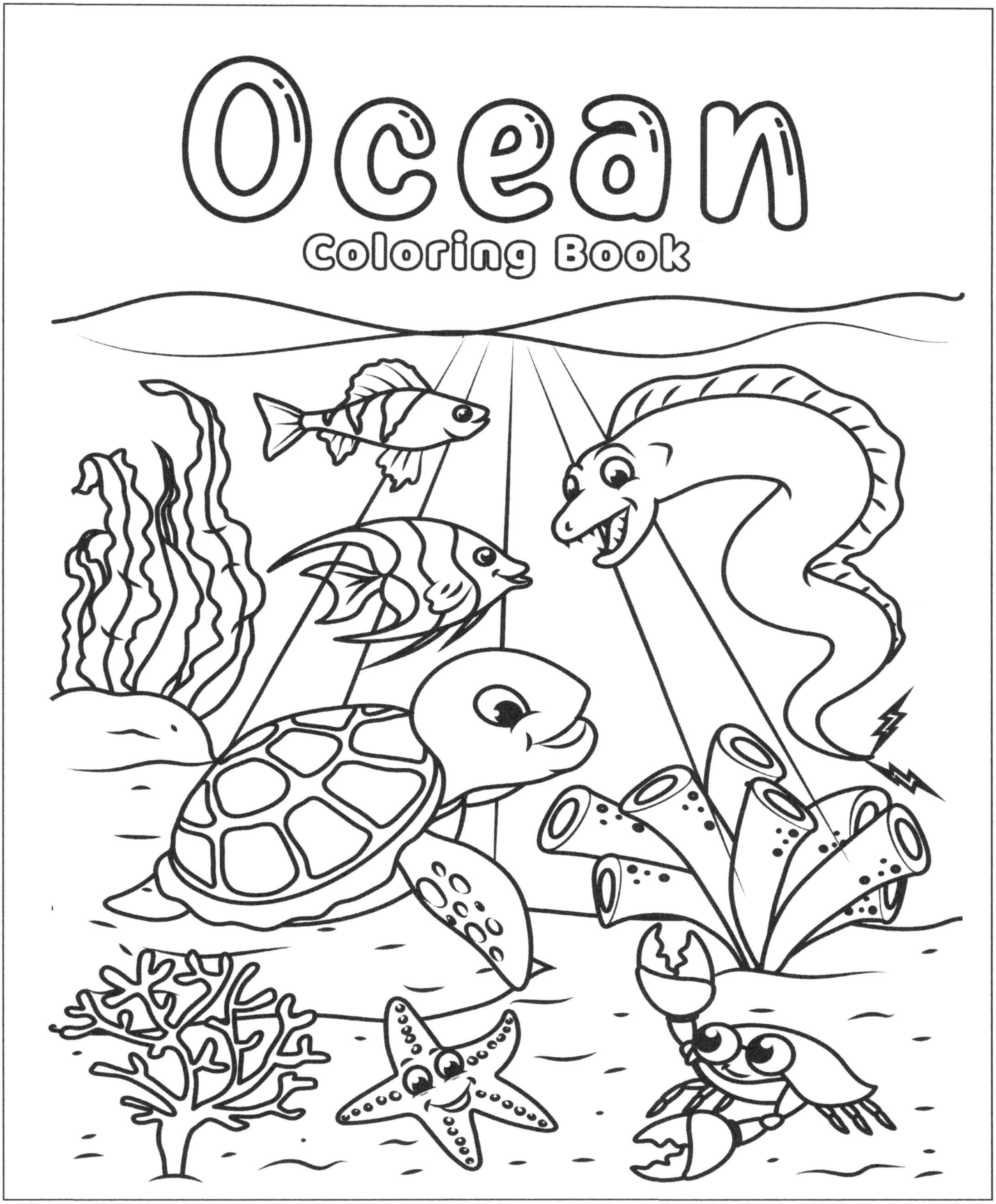

Made in the USA
Las Vegas, NV
25 March 2024

87759240R00057